ENDORSEMENTS

"*Gospel in the Home* is an excellent resource for churches and families. The authors present a fresh look at how biblical principles can strengthen familial relationships and keep homes resilient in our post-Christian culture. The theological foundations of the home are taught with clarity, and the applications are easily understood. This book will have a strong influence on our Christian community for years to come. Thank you, Connor and Todd!"

—Susie Hawkins
Author and National Speaker

"What a timely book for our culture today! In *Gospel in the Home*, Todd and Connor weave together biblical truths and humorous life stories to remind us that our families desperately need the gospel to be the center of all that we do and say. Every family should read and apply these principles immediately!"

—Nathan Lorick
Director of Evangelism
Southern Baptists of Texas Convention

"Todd and Connor have done the Church a great favor in writing to implore believers of the need and urgency to make Christ and his gospel preeminent in the home. While the family is continually under attack and attempting to be redefined, this book provides hope and encouragement. *Gospel in the Home* is a great resource for building godly families and I recommend it for both personal reading and small group study."

—Dr. Jarrett Stephens
Teaching Pastor
Prestonwood Baptist Church

GOSPEL in the HOME
turning chaos back into order

Connor Bales and Todd Kaunitz

LUCIDBOOKS

Gospel in the Home
Copyright © 2016 by Connor Bales and Todd Kaunitz

Published by Lucid Books in Houston, TX.
www.LucidBooks.net

All rights reserved. No part of this publication may be reproduced, stored in a retrieval system, or transmitted in any form by any means, electronic, mechanical, photocopy, recording, or otherwise, without the prior permission of the publisher, except as provided for by USA copyright law.

Scripture quotations are from the ESV® Bible (The Holy Bible, English Standard Version®), copyright © 2001 by Crossway, a publishing ministry of Good News Publishers. Used by permission. All rights reserved.

First Printing 2016

ISBN 10: 1-63296-090-7
ISBN 13: 978-1-63296-090-0
eISBN 10: 1-63296-091-5
eISBN: 978-1-63296-091-7

Special Sales: Most Lucid Books titles are available in special quantity discounts. Custom imprinting or excerpting can also be done to fit special needs. Contact Lucid Books at info@lucidbooks.net.

We would like to dedicate this book to
our wives and families.
Thank you to both Adrian and Mary
for your unconditional love and support
and for faithfully displaying
the gospel of grace to us every day.

TABLE OF CONTENTS

Foreword vii

Introduction 1

One: Broken Together 11

Two: His 29

Three: Hers 49

Four: Redeeming Intimacy 69

Five: Be Fruitful and Multiply 89

Six: For Richer, for Poorer 109

Seven: A Single Purpose 133

Eight: The New Normal 155

FOREWORD

In serving as a pastor for nearly five decades now, I have witnessed firsthand the remarkable changes that have taken place through the years as it relates to families and the home. When I was growing up, I knew of only one or two kids in my elementary school whose parents went through a divorce. Promiscuity may have been practiced, but it was certainly kept secret and subjects like pornography and homosexuality were rarely brought up or mentioned.

Fast-forward to today and we are seeing the negative effects of the cultural assault on the sanctity of marriage as well as the destruction of the traditional family. What's the answer?

Some suggest it's in politics and in the establishment of new laws. Others warn that we are past the point of no return and with the reinvention of marriage, the home will never be the same. What is the answer to the systematic attack and breakdown of the home today?

I believe it's provided in the title of Todd Kaunitz and Connor Bales' book, *Gospel in the Home*. As simple as it may sound, the gospel really is the answer. Husbands will lead faithfully only when Christ is in the center of their lives and they are following his example. Wives will serve and love their husbands well, only when Christ is in the center of their lives and they are following his example. Moms and dads can parent well only when Christ is at the center of their marriage and has his place of preeminence in the home.

The way marriages can endure and families can go the distance is to put the gospel in the home.

From discussing men's and women's roles in the marriage to communication to raising children to discussing subjects like intimacy and singleness, Todd and Connor offer biblical insight to help navigate serious issues that are causing conflict and creating chaos in marriages and in homes.

Combining personal stories with humor, wise counsel and practical application, anyone who reads this book will walk away challenged in their faith and encouraged in their marriage.

What I appreciate most about this book is that it is written from the perspective of two local church pastors who are attempting to answer questions their congregation and the culture around them is asking. Rather than dancing around sensitive topics and in no way compromising the truth of Scripture, they address head on the need for repentance, grace and total surrender to Christ.

Whether you are about to be married, newly married, been married for years or about to give up on your marriage, this book can help. It offers hope and can bring healing when read with a humble spirit and soft heart. May God bless, strengthen and restore the *Gospel in the Home*.

—Dr. Jack Graham
Sr. Pastor, Prestonwood Baptist Church

INTRODUCTION

The last thing we want is for you to think this book is about trying harder. It's not.

Trying harder is not what relationships are about.
Trying harder is not what your best future is about.
Trying harder is definitely not what the gospel is about.

We've learned this in our own lives, and ironically, we've often learned it the hard way—by trying harder. For many years, we thought the Christian life was about checking all the right boxes.

So, we understand why a lot of people avoid or distrust church, or just mentally check out—because they associate church with a list of things to do and not do. If that's how you approach faith and life, you'll soon be running on empty. Maybe you already are.

We have good news for you: "Gospel" literally means *good news*. It does not mean, *Try harder and maybe you'll get it right eventually*.

Jesus never said, "I have come that you might have life and have it abundantly *by trying harder*."

And there's no such verse in the Bible as: "For God so loved the world, that he gave his only Son, that whoever believes in him should not perish but have eternal life *by trying harder*."

Don't get us wrong. We believe in hard work. We believe in commitment. But what we're talking about in this book is rooted in love—God's unconditional love, which cannot be earned by any amount of human effort. This love is where the gospel begins. And it's why trying harder is not the point.

• • •

If you don't know already, y'all are going to find out soon enough that we are both from the South. We come from the land of *fellas* and *ladies* who mind their manners and say *yes sir* and *yes ma'am*.

Another thing about the South—church is a big deal. We grew up in church. But we know from personal experience that church doesn't guarantee you'll "get it" when it comes to the gospel. As kids, we both mixed up the message somehow.

So, as we introduce this book, we're also going to introduce ourselves. We're going to share our discovery of what the gospel means in everyday life. In doing so, we invite you to consider your life and relationships in light of the gospel—maybe for the first time.

Connor: Coming to Jesus on a cattle ranch.

I guess a cattle ranch is as good a place as any for a come-to-Jesus moment. And that's where I was the summer of my junior year of college, working as a ranch hand in Salida, Colorado.

Now, cattle ranchers take the long view on managing their land and livestock. It's a way of life. Ignore a problem one year, and it's likely to come back bigger the next.

For example, if certain kinds of brush are left to grow, they can take over a pasture. They draw down the water supply and reduce nearby streams to a trickle. They choke out better

Introduction

varieties of vegetation. They become a wildfire waiting to happen.

That pretty much describes my life up to age 21. I had been raised in the things of God (and for that I am grateful), but I only evidenced my belief in Jesus in external facades. Internally, I battled sin and rebellion as if wild brush had taken root and gained ground.

Early one morning at the ranch, I remember feeling frustrated with life—and it showed. The ranch owner, a Christian man, could see that I was carrying a chip on my shoulder. Over a discipleship breakfast he called out my bad attitude. He challenged me to think about my life and in a very firm and loving way, truly questioned whether or not I had surrendered my life to what I said I believed.

Later that day, all by myself in the middle of a cow pasture, I cried out loud to God. *I'm unhappy, and I don't know why. Please help me. Please save me.* The Lord brought me to my knees right then and there, and I was born again.

I had a great upbringing with lots of gospel conversation. My parents instilled the truth of faith in Christ from a very early age, yet I had made it an external gospel. I had made it about appearances, rather than surrender to Christ. Jesus saved my life in 1998 and while it took me years to truly discover what "life in Christ" looked like, I have never been the same since.

....

We keep up appearances because we want life to be better than it is. And we want our relationships to be better than they are. So we keep trying harder, and even if things are not going well, we put on a good front. Sadly, Christians are notorious for this.

But it doesn't matter whether or not you grew up in church. It doesn't matter whether you're a skeptic, a spiritual seeker, or a faithful follower of Jesus. The benefit you receive from this book doesn't depend on how much you know or believe about God, the Bible, or the gospel.

Just come as you are.

Are you doing okay in your relationships but afraid you'll screw up?
Are you tired of trying harder and feeling like it's not enough?
Are you eager to make your life count for something?

Come as you are.
Are you a hot mess?
Even so, come as you are. And don't worry, because the good news of the gospel begins with the bad news of the human condition: All of us are messed up.

We can never be fully alive in our own power, no matter how hard we try.

Deep in our souls, we are messed up. Despite our best intentions, we are flawed, selfish, and sometimes downright awful and evil. And guess what? This human condition is the reality for all of us. Nobody is exempt. Nobody can claim innocence.

It's like when you're watching a movie, and you can tell where the plot is headed. There's an expression when you see a character you know is doomed: *He's a dead man.* In the scene you're watching, he is alive and breathing, but there's no question about his fate. Nothing he can do will save him.

The Bible uses this same expression to describe humanity before the gospel entered the picture: *Dead.* Here's how Ephesians 2:1 to 3 puts it:

And you were dead in the trespasses and sins in which you once walked, following the course of this world, following the prince of the power of the air, the spirit that is now at work in the

Introduction

sons of disobedience—among whom we all once lived in the passions of our flesh, carrying out the desires of the body and the mind, and were by nature children of wrath, like the rest of mankind.

This is the bad news of the human condition. When we see sin and suffering in the world around us, it is the stench of death.

All the pain.
All the tragedy.
All the injustice.

This is the foul odor of a fate we cannot escape. And it's not only a physical reality, it's a spiritual reality too. We're under a death sentence. We cannot save ourselves.

Many people put on the perfume of religion, trying to overpower evil with good. They try to clean themselves up and make themselves better. But the gospel is not about bad people who need to get better, it's about dead people who need resurrected new life.

....

Todd: Coming to Terms with Death

My first close encounter with death came when I was 16 years old and one of my very best friends was killed in a car crash. I felt all the normal emotions that a person feels when losing someone you love at such a young age, but the most overwhelming truth that hit me was that of my own mortality. It forced me to come to terms with a reality I couldn't escape, "I am going to to die one day!" I had such an uncertainty about where I would spend eternity.

Never mind my religious reasons to feel secure. They were gone.

It didn't matter that I had told myself that I was "good with

God" because my family was active in church and that I wasn't as bad as some people I knew.

It didn't matter that I had been raised in church and immersed in Christian culture, or that I was familiar with the gospel and knew a lot about Jesus.

My friend's death shattered my worldview.

Until then, I had been looking for identity and significance in foolish choices that were fleeting and only led to greater hopelessness. I pursued friends, sports, and girls. But I still felt like something was missing from my life.

The Friday night after the accident, I had planned to go out with friends and have a good time—you know, the kind of good time that's typically bad news.

Instead, I went to a revival service that night. The pastor preached the gospel, and I realized for the first time that I was spiritually dead and that Jesus was my only hope. I got on my knees and gave my life to Jesus, and the Holy Spirit made me alive in an instant!

It took many years after that for me to understand the gospel in everyday life. I spent a lot of time after my salvation thinking that I needed to compensate for the choices I had made. But as I have grown in the gospel, now I know that it frees me from the guilt and shame. I now rest in the finished work of Jesus—and I want that for you too.

....

With all this talk of death, you may be wondering, *What about God's love? What about goodness and grace?* That's coming, so hang on. There's good news ahead.

But listen, if God is *good*, he has to deal with *bad*. All of it. Every little bit. You may not be an axe murderer, but you aren't perfect either. There's a bit of a bad in all of us. The Bible calls this sin.

Introduction

Think about how you react to poverty, disease, and human trafficking. *We've got do something about this.* It just isn't fair when bad seems to be getting the upper hand over good.

Even a smaller injustice can get your attention. For example, let's say your paycheck is $100 less than it should be. You could say, *Oh well, people make mistakes. I'll just let it go.* More likely, you're going to point out the mistake and make sure it gets reconciled. That's only fair. That's justice.

Whether the sin is great or small, a good and just God must pay attention. He must reconcile the injustice. And this is where the good news comes in. Let's continue reading Ephesians 2:4 to 6:

> **But God, being rich in mercy, because of the great love with which he loved us, even when we were dead in our trespasses, made us alive together with Christ—by grace you have been saved—and raised us up with him and seated us with him in the heavenly places in Christ Jesus. . . .**

Did you catch those two little words that change everything for humanity? *But God.*

You were dead . . . But God.

The tragedy of the human condition is not the end of the story. The gospel doesn't ignore sin. The gospel confronts sin head-on. We are helpless to save ourselves, but because of God's mercy and grace, we are not hopeless. We were dead, but now can be redeemed and resurrected to new life with Christ.

We can be fully redeemed by God's grace, no matter what we have done.

Throughout this book, we will explore what redeemed life and redeemed relationships look like—in other words, how to live in light of the gospel. But first, we want to outline the foundational promise of the gospel for you, rooted in God's unconditional love. Don't miss this, or you'll miss the point of the whole book.

God doesn't love you because of what you do or don't do.
That would be conditional.

God simply loves you. Period.
That's unconditional.

God is rich in mercy and grace toward you. At the same time, he is righteous and holy and cannot ignore sin.

Yes, you are guilty of sin—a reality of the human condition.
But God.

Yes, sin comes with the sentence of death. You cannot escape it.
But God.

No, you cannot save yourself.
But God.

By sending Jesus Christ to die on the cross for the sin of the world, God made a way to redeem you. No matter what you have done—a little bit bad, or a lot—God's grace covers sin so that the sentence of death gives way to the promise of being made alive with Christ. And though your earthly life will someday end, your spiritual life with Christ can begin now and last forever.

Why would God do this? Why would he offer you this kind of life? Ephesians 2:7 tells us:

. . . so that in the coming ages he might show the immeasurable riches of his grace in kindness toward us in Christ Jesus.

Introduction

God did this so that your life would be a display of his grace and mercy. So that your relationships would be a display of his grace and mercy too.

Think about a trophy and the victory it represents. Do you celebrate the trophy itself? No. You celebrate the one who accomplished the victory.

Your life can be a trophy of God's grace. When people see your life and relationships redeemed from death to life, they will see the greatness and the grandeur of God. It displays the victory that God accomplished through Christ.

Here's the thing: A trophy cannot try harder to win the victory. It's impossible. You cannot achieve God's grace by trying harder. You can only accept it. Look at what Ephesians 2:8 to 9 says:

For by grace you have been saved through faith. And this is not your own doing; it is the gift of God, not a result of works, so that no one may boast.

The gift of God. Have you accepted this gift of God? Let today be the day you say yes to the gospel. Let today be the day you put your faith in God, through Jesus Christ, the only one who can save you. You can pause right now and say this prayer:

Lord Jesus Christ, I am a sinner in need of a Savior. I ask you to do for me what I cannot do for myself. Forgive my sin and cover me in your grace. You are my only hope. I want to be made alive in you. Amen.

The hope of the gospel begins now, as you become a living, breathing trophy of God's grace in your everyday life and relationships. In the chapters to come, you're going to see in very practical terms how the gospel changes everything.

Gospel in the Home

The gospel in marriage and singleness.
The gospel in identity and intimacy.
The gospel in family and finances.
The gospel in the home.

And it's not about trying harder. As we see in Ephesians 2:10, it's about being who God made you to be:

For we are his workmanship, created in Christ Jesus for good works, which God prepared beforehand, that we should walk in them.

Are you ready to get going?

• • •

If you prayed to accept God's gift of life in Christ, we'd like to be the first to welcome you to the family. To help you grow in Christ, we encourage you to make three commitments to yourself.

1. Tell another Christian about your new spiritual life—perhaps a friend, family member, or local pastor. If you don't know another Christian, email us at New Beginnings Church: GITH @nbbctx.org. We would love to hear from you.

2. Find a Bible-believing, gospel-centered, Jesus-exalting church near you. This will help you grow in Christ, connect in relationships, and learn more about the Bible. Every church community is unique, so it may take a few tries to get the right fit.

3. Finish reading this book. We figure you were planning to do that anyway, so go ahead. We're excited for you to discover the life God has for you.

One

BROKEN TOGETHER

Imagine you could go back in time and strike up a conversation with the inventor of the bicycle. As you approach him, you can tell he takes great pleasure in seeing people enjoy his invention. With pedals, tires, handlebars, and a seat or two, people go places faster and farther than they ever could on foot. Riding a bicycle is fun. And who doesn't remember the sense of pride when it's finally time to take the training wheels off? It's a rite of passage.

So, you say to the inventor, "Oh, I know what *that* is. That's a bicycle. I've got one, and I've got my own way of riding it. I sit on it facing backwards and hop up and down to make it go. It's not as easy as I'd hoped, but I'm working at it."

The inventor looks astonished. "Why don't you try riding the bicycle in the way I've designed it to work? You sit facing forward, put your feet on the pedals, grab the handlebars, and move your legs. That's how you make it go."

"Thanks," you say, "but I'll just keep trying it my way. I'm sure I can get better with practice." And before long, you give up.

People say marriage isn't working.
It's broken.
It's antiquated.
It's time to redefine it for the modern world.

Actually, we've missed what the inventor had in mind. We've attempted to redefine something we didn't design, and now we're frustrated because it's not working. The problem is not a design flaw.

Marriage isn't broken, people are. And when broken people get married, they're simply broken together—riding the wrong way on a bicycle built for two.

• • •

In case your personal experience hasn't revealed for you the mess that America's marriages are in today, the disturbing statistics tell the story:

- 60 percent of men and women move in together prior to their first marriage.[1]
- Among adults who have been married, 33 percent have been divorced, which equates to 25 percent of all adults over the age of 18.[2]

George Barna, who reported these statistics[3], summarized the trends identified in his research:

---

1. http://www.cdc.gov/nchs/data/nhsr/nhsr049.pdf

2. https://www.barna.org/barna-update/family-kids/42-new-marriage-and-divorce-statistics-released#.VcpZJs6m3Uk

3. Slight fact check: It appears to me that the first statistic comes from the CDC, and only the second one comes from Barna.

There no longer seems to be much of a stigma attached to divorce; it is now seen as an unavoidable rite of passage. Interviews with young adults suggest that they want their initial marriage to last but are not particularly optimistic about that possibility. There is also evidence that many young people are moving toward embracing the idea of serial marriage, in which a person gets married two or three times, seeking a different partner for each phase of their adult life.[4]

How sad. But also how true in revealing our brokenness, to the point that people have given up the hope of a lasting marriage. They don't believe it's possible.

Unfortunately, things don't look any better when we measure the impact of brokenness on family life:

- 12 million parents are going it alone, without a spouse, and more than 80 percent of them are single moms.[5]
- More than 17 million children—one out of every four—are being raised without a dad.[6]

To say things aren't working perfectly is an understatement. We are broken people, and the state of marriage unmasks us for who we really are.

---

4. https://www.barna.org/barna-update/family-kids/42-new-marriage-and-divorce-statistics-released#.VcpZJs6m3Uk
5. https://singlemotherguide.com/single-mother-statistics/
6. https://singlemotherguide.com/single-mother-statistics/

Connor: Our Honeymoon Wake-up Call

Mary and I had just gotten back from our honeymoon and were settling into our first apartment as a married couple.

One Sunday afternoon, she called her mom in Houston. As they were talking, her mom asked a string of questions: "How's married life? Are y'all adjusting? Did you get your wedding gifts unpacked? Are you settled in from your honeymoon?"

Mary didn't exactly answer. She just said, "He never leaves." And with that, she started crying. "He's there when I wake up. He's there when I go to bed. He never leaves."

Her mom laughed and said, "Welcome to marriage," and hung up the phone.

Then Mary picked up the phone and called *my* mother. The two of them had the same conversation. My mom responded by laughing too, and she said, "Honey, you can't give him back."

That was a wake-up call for Mary. You can bet it was for me too. The honeymoon was over, and we began to learn what it means to be broken together.

A Love Story Before Brokenness

Statistics tell us that relationships in our society are broken. Our marriage experience tells us that we as people are broken. But once upon a time, before brokenness, there was a love story to show us what wholeness looked like.

God's Word tells us this love story in Genesis chapters 1 and 2. The first chapter tells the creation story. The second uses an ancient literary technique called an *echo* to flesh out the same story in greater detail; that's where the creation story becomes a love story.

As we read both chapters, we see that humanity is the pinnacle of God's creation. We are made in God's image, after his likeness, and for the purpose of revealing his glory. Let's look at Genesis 2:19 to 20:

> Now out of the ground the LORD God had formed every beast of the field and every bird of the heavens and brought them to the man to see what he would call them. And whatever the man called every living creature, that was its name. The man gave names to all livestock and to the birds of the heavens and to every beast of the field. But for Adam there was not found a helper fit for him.

God had given Adam the role of stewarding—or caring for—creation. So Adam named all the creatures and studied them. As he did so, he came to the realization that he was the only creature who didn't have an equal counterpart. Something, someone, was missing. We continue the story in verses 21 to 23:

> So the LORD God caused a deep sleep to fall upon the man, and while he slept took one of his ribs and closed up its place with flesh. And the rib that the LORD God had taken from the man he made into a woman and brought her to the man. Then the man said,
>
> "This at last is bone of my bones
>   and flesh of my flesh;
> she shall be called Woman,
>   because she was taken out of Man."

Did you notice the lyrics of Adam's love song? What a hopeless romantic. He was overjoyed. Then, just as he had named all the creatures, Adam named his counterpart: Eve.

As we continue to explore Genesis 1 through 2 in light of the whole Bible, we discover that this creation love story reveals how marriage is meant to be.

God alone is the designer of marriage.

The first thing we discover in the story of Adam and Eve is God's design for marriage. Their relationship was not an accident. It was not coincidental. It was not the result of some cosmic energy, but rather the work of God's very own hand.

As the Creator of both Adam and Eve—Man and Woman—God alone is the designer of the relationship they enjoy together. And in the time before brokenness, their relationship was perfect.

You can see the perfection in Genesis 2:25: "And the man and his wife were both naked and were not ashamed." Being naked meant being open and vulnerable and fully known. But with no shame. No strife. No abuse. No unmet expectations. Rather, Adam and Eve enjoyed a holy union designed by God.

With all the problems in our world today, we can hardly picture this perfection:

Marriage by God's design is simply one man and one woman in a lifelong covenant relationship, who live in fellowship together while stewarding the creation and enjoying the Creator.

If that's God's design, and yet it doesn't match our experience, then we are left to ask: *What happened? What went wrong?*

....

Todd: The Perfect Husband for Mrs. Right

I was the weird guy growing up. All my friends had the mindset to get out of college, start a career, and then maybe establish a family.

But in high school, I thought: *No, I'm getting married as soon as possible. I'm going to find Mrs. Right and marry her. We're going to have kids, and it's going to be awesome.*

My idealistic view of marriage was simple: The perfect woman married to the perfect man—me. We would laugh all the time. We'd never argue. Sex would happen frequently, and it would always be amazing, and we'd never have bad breath the morning after.

I'm sure you can think of a few problems with my view of marriage. Here's the biggest one: I am not the perfect man. Once I entered into the marriage relationship, I realized how very self-centered and immature I was. Marriage revealed the brokenness in my heart.

....

We long for a good marriage. But as husband and wife, we come face to face with our imperfections—literally. And we wonder where things went wrong. The problem isn't a flawed *design*. It's that we haven't fulfilled the design in the way God alone *defines*.

God alone is the definer of marriage.

At a wedding ceremony—possibly your own—you may have heard the minister say: "Therefore shall a man *leave* his father and his mother, and shall *cleave* unto his wife: and they shall be one flesh." Leave and cleave. That's the language of Genesis 2:24 in the King James Version of the Bible, translated during the time of Shakespeare. It sounds so *Romeo and Juliet*.

Cleave is an unfamiliar word to us now. It implies a *covenant*. That's another word we don't use much. But the meaning of these words is essential to understanding God's definition of marriage. In the Hebrew language of the Old Testament, *cleave* means to be glued to something. Elsewhere in the Bible, *cleave* means to unite with someone through a covenant, which is a binding promise or oath.

As God defines it, marriage was always meant to be a covenant. But in our world—a world where divorce seems like a rite of passage and serial marriage is a foregone conclusion—we treat marriage like a *contract*.

What's the difference between a covenant and a contract?

A covenant is binding, but a contract is conditional.
A covenant is based on giving, but a contract is based on receiving.
A covenant is about serving, but a contract is about being served.
A covenant says, *I will*, but a contract says, *I will if you do*.

In his book, *The Mingling of Souls*, Matt Chandler describes the commitment required in a covenant marriage:

It's not fifty-fifty; it's one hundred-one hundred. At any given time either spouse won't have 100 percent to give, but this does not diminish the other's commitment because they are not in a contract but a covenant. As in the covenant of grace initiated by God to save sinners, one party can give 100 percent even if the other gives nothing.[7]

In Jesus, God established a covenant with us. It is not dependent upon our performance. It is not dependent upon how much we give. In fact, hold up the universal hand-sign for zero. That's how much we contribute to our salvation in Jesus. Zero percent. Yet, Jesus pursues us 100 percent. In our contract world, getting something for nothing is too good to be true. But with God, it's true. With a covenant, it's true.

In marriage, a covenant doesn't make sense unless you understand that God's design is for your spouse to hold the highest place in your human relationships.

---

7. Matt Chandler, *The Mingling of Souls* (Colorado Springs, CO: David C. Cook, 2015), 104.

Let's go back to the story of Adam and Eve, to the question we haven't addressed yet: *What went wrong?* The short answer is what we call the Fall. You've probably heard the expression, "fall from grace." Well, Genesis is where it happened for all of humanity.

We read in Genesis 2:17 that God gave one command to Adam: "but of the tree of the knowledge of good and evil you shall not eat, for in the day that you eat of it you shall surely die." But in chapter 3, we see that Satan, God's Enemy, showed up and tempted Adam and Eve to eat from that very tree.

Adam and Eve chose to disobey one command. How do you mess that up? But they did. They put their own fulfillment ahead of God's design. That's called sin. And sin fractured everything God had created in perfect harmony. Sin broke the wholeness that the Hebrew language calls *shalom*. Adam and Eve were naked, and now sin left them feeling ashamed. Look at the consequences in Genesis 3:16 to 19:

> **To the woman he said,**
>
> **"I will surely multiply your pain in childbearing;**
> ** in pain you shall bring forth children.**
> **Your desire shall be for your husband,**
> ** and he shall rule over you."**
>
> **And to Adam he said,**
>
> **"Because you have listened to the voice of your wife**
> ** and have eaten of the tree**
> **of which I commanded you,**
> ** 'You shall not eat of it,'**
> **cursed is the ground because of you;**
> ** in pain you shall eat of it all the days of your life;**
> **thorns and thistles it shall bring forth for you;**
> ** and you shall eat the plants of the field.**

> **By the sweat of your face**
>   **you shall eat bread,**
> **till you return to the ground,**
>   **for out of it you were taken;**
> **for you are dust,**
>   **and to dust you shall return."**

The consequences of sin hit home. Through Adam and Eve, the Fall forever changed the human experience of marriage and family relationships—not for better, but for worse.

....

Todd: The 159-Mile Argument

When Adrian and I were newly married, I remember the dumb fights we had. We often argued about Thanksgiving and Christmas—whose family to visit first and which traditions to make a priority. Sound familiar?

During one holiday road trip, we fought for 159 miles from Longview, Texas all the way to Camden, Arkansas. As we pulled onto the oil-top road near the little city where I grew up, we had to call the family and tell them which side we were going to visit first.

"I'm not calling. You're calling!" I shot first. Then she shot back to me.

We only had one cell phone at the time, so as we argued, we passed it back and forth like a hot potato. And I don't know why, but I decided to settle the argument by throwing the phone out the window. You can guess how well that worked. So I put the car in reverse, went back to find the phone in the woods along the road, and then got back in the car.

Silence. The loud kind.

Finally she said, "You're a moron." And as if I needed to hear it again, *"You're a moron."*

The truth is, she was right—not only about me, but about all of us. In our sin, we make selfish and stupid choices even though we know better.

....

While we see clearly that God is the designer of humanity and the definer of marriage, we also see how sin has broken the beauty he intended. As the story of Adam and Eve continues, God is not finished yet. He is a covenant God, remember? He says *I will,* not *I will if you do.* Our brokenness does not cancel his commitment. But all of humanity must deal with the consequences of sin.

God alone is the redeemer of brokenness.

We live with fallout from the Fall. The curse we've already read from Genesis 3 provides a grim picture, not at all like the perfection God designed. Due to the sin of Adam and Eve, we face four kinds of consequences that affect our marriage relationships.

1. **Marriage is filled with friction.** We now possess a sinful nature. And guess what that means in the home? Two sinners are going to sin against each other. When God says to Eve, "Your desire will be for your husband," some scholars believe this means the wife will live in an unhealthy subservient role to her husband. Other scholars interpret that the wife will war against the position God has given the husband in the home.

    Regardless of the interpretation, there are going to be problems in the marriage relationship. Rather than serving his wife in love, and leading life at home in that spirit, the husband is going to lord his position over the wife. So there will be chaos where once there was peace. *Shalom* has been broken.

2. **Parenting is painful.** God tells Eve that childbearing will be painful. The meaning here includes not only the childbirth, but also to the raising of the children. When you have two sinful people who conceive a child together, guess what? They're going to give birth to a sinful child. Just look at Genesis chapter 4, and you'll find the story of sibling rivalry between two brothers, Cain and Abel. In jealousy, Cain killed Abel. That's about as painful as it gets.

3. **Life's labor and responsibilities are difficult.** God created work before the Fall, in the perfection of Eden. For example, Adam had the job of stewarding creation and naming all the animals. So, work itself is not a curse. But now, rather than being a joy, work requires toil and sweat. Now, instead of Adam working the earth, the earth is going to work against Adam. There will be thistles and thorns. For us, that means making ends meet is difficult. We worry about finances, and work adds stress to our lives.

4. **Humanity's relationship with God has been severed.** When God told Adam he would die if he ate from the forbidden tree, God was not only referring to physical death, but also spiritual death. As the story unfolds in Genesis 3, God banishes Adam and Eve from the Garden of Eden, from the source of life. They can no longer enjoy fellowship with God as they once did.

Every one of us was created to enjoy fellowship with God. Like Adam and Eve, we were made in his image to display his glory as we walk with him. But with the Fall, our relationship with God has been severed. Therefore, on a spiritual level, we lack the kind of purpose and fulfillment that can only be found in relationship with God. Instead of looking to our Creator as the source of our satisfaction, we look elsewhere. Often, we expect our spouse or others to fill the void.

As a married person, maybe you can relate. Maybe you've had thoughts like, *I feel so unfulfilled. I'm not getting what I need from my marriage.* The fulfillment you're missing was never meant to be provided by your spouse. It was meant to be provided by God. When you look to your spouse to do for you what only God can do, you will eventually destroy your marriage relationship. Your spouse and family will be crushed under the weight of impossible expectations.

As a single person, perhaps you express similar desires in a different way. Perhaps you've thought, *I have to get married. Something is missing, but when I find the one for me, then I'll feel complete.* Don't be fooled by that line from *Jerry McGuire:* "You complete me." It only happens in the movies.

In real life, if you look to marriage to fill the spiritual void you feel, you'll eventually be disappointed. No human being can complete you. Only the God who created you can complete you.

The Love Story After Brokenness

The lack of fulfillment you feel comes from a longing to be loved. Your spouse—or lack of one—is not the problem. Your family is not the problem. Sin is the problem, and the root of it goes all the way back to the moment when Adam and Eve chose to go against God's command. They felt shame for the first time. Instead of experiencing intimacy with each other and with God, they felt naked and exposed. So they used fig leaves to cover themselves.

Those fig leaves would provide temporary cover but eventually wither and fade away. That's what happens when we try to hide our shame. We can't cover it for very long. But look at Genesis 3:21: "And the Lord God made for Adam and for his wife garments of skins and clothed them."

God essentially said, *I will provide a covering. I will clothe humanity, which I have created.*

So, God took the life of one of the very creatures Adam had named. Blood was shed—not to remove the consequences, but to make a covering for the guilt and shame of sin. This scene in the garden of Eden illustrates what God ultimately did for us in Jesus Christ. It is the good news of the gospel, in which God says to us: *Yes, you're broken. Yes, you're sinful. But I will provide a way to redeem you.*

The blood of Jesus Christ was shed to cover the guilt and shame of your sin. This is the shelter of grace, your home in the gospel and the only power to get the gospel in your home.

• • •

Let's turn to the New Testament, to the book of Ephesians. In chapter 1, we see what God had in view when he designed and defined marriage. Verses 7 to 10 describe the salvation that is ours to accept in Jesus Christ:

In him we have redemption through his blood, the forgiveness of our trespasses, according to the riches of his grace, which he lavished upon us, in all wisdom and insight making known to us the mystery of his will, according to his purpose, which he set forth in Christ as a plan for the fullness of time, to unite all things in him, things in heaven and things on earth.

You may be thinking, *What does this have to do with marriage?* Good question. Notice two words at the end of verse 10: *all things.* God is in the business of redeeming all things. That means your marriage is not too far gone. Your family is not too dysfunctional. You are not beyond hope.

This is the glory of the gospel: God loves us so much that he has made a way to redeem all that is wrong with us, including our broken attempts to live out his good and glorious design for marriage.

Broken Together

The primary meaning of marriage is to illustrate the gospel.

Contrary to popular opinion, marriage is not all about our happiness. At times we may find great happiness in it. But in his grace, God has defined marriage to illustrate the gospel. We find the deeper meaning of marriage in Ephesians 5:31 to 33, where the apostle Paul quotes from Genesis 2:24:

> "Therefore a man shall leave his father and mother and hold fast to his wife, and the two shall become one flesh." This mystery is profound, and I am saying that it refers to Christ and the church. However, let each one of you love his wife as himself, and let the wife see that she respects her husband.

That word *mystery* is significant. In the Greek language it's *megas musterion*—mega-mystery. This is not a crime-solving kind of mystery. Think bigger than that. Something is going on beyond natural understanding. More than just the union of husband and wife, marriage represents the covenant between Jesus Christ and his bride: the redeemed people of God, the church.

Tim Keller says it this way in his book, *The Meaning of Marriage:* "This is the secret—that the gospel of Jesus and marriage explain one another. That when God invented marriage, he already had the saving work of Jesus in mind."[8]

If you're looking for the secret to a meaningful marriage, this is it. We are unworthy of love, and yet we have experienced the unconditional love of God who says *I will,* not *I will if you do.* That's the vow of a covenant. *I will. I do.* No conditions.

---

8. Timothy Keller, *The Meaning of Marriage* (New York, NY: Penguin, 2013), 43.

Each of us is to love our spouse with this kind of covenant commitment. Not because either one has earned it or deserves it. But because when we show that kind of love in our marriage, we illustrate the unconditional love we have experienced in God, through Jesus Christ.

The path to a meaningful marriage is to imitate the gospel.

Until the unconditional love demonstrated in the gospel takes hold of our hearts, we won't experience the meaningful marriage God desires for us. And who wants anything less? But too often, we look for love in someone or something else. We disregard God's design and try to ride through life our own way, backwards on the bicycle.

Consequently, we have to reorient ourselves and find the path to a meaningful marriage by imitating the gospel. This does not mean "fake it till you make it," as the saying goes. This kind of imitation means following the model of God's love toward us. We see that model in 1 John 4:7 to 11:

> **Beloved, let us love one another, for love is from God, and whoever loves has been born of God and knows God. Anyone who does not love does not know God, because God is love. In this the love of God was made manifest among us, that God sent his only Son into the world, so that we might live through him. In this is love, not that we have loved God but that he loved us and sent his Son to be the propitiation for our sins. Beloved, if God so loved us, we also ought to love one another.**

In love, God initiated a relationship with us, no strings attached. We are to love one another the same way.

In Matthew 22:36 to 39, Jesus was asked what is the greatest commandment. He replied: "Love the Lord your God with all your heart and with all your soul and with all your mind." Then Jesus goes on to the second commandment, "Love your neighbor as yourself."

Your neighbors are the people who live close to you. You can probably guess who your number-one neighbor is, right? Your spouse. And next, your children. Your closest neighbors live in your very own home. So, living out the commandment of love begins in your own household. When you learn to express God's unconditional love toward your spouse and children, you reflect his unconditional love toward you. That's the gospel in the home.

• • •

What if this kind of love could become like breathing? With each inhale and exhale, you think about the radical grace of God you have experienced in your life. The unconditional love. The forgiveness of sin made possible through Jesus Christ.

Breathe in God's grace.

Then consider the closest relationships he has entrusted to you. Breathe out God's grace on them.

As a husband, you might be thinking, *You don't know what she's like—how she frustrates me.* But do you deserve God's unconditional love any more than her?

Breathe in God's grace.
Breathe out God's grace.

As a wife, you might be thinking, *You don't understand how he treats me and takes me for granted.* Well, do you deserve God's compassion any more than him?

Breathe in God's mercy.
Breathe out God's mercy.

Gospel in the Home

As a single person, whether you've never married, or you're divorced, you might be thinking, *You don't know the longing I carry in my heart.* But will you open yourself to the fulfillment God longs to show you?

Breathe in God's love.
Breathe out God's love.

If you are enjoying a healthy marriage, then be thankful that God has partnered you with someone who loves you despite yourself. That's grace. That's mercy.

Breathe in.
Breathe out.

We are broken people. And in marriage, we are broken together. Still, in marriage designed, defined, and redeemed by God, we see an illustration of God's covenant with us, in Jesus Christ, so that we can imitate the grace of the gospel in the home.

Creator God,
We love you, and we thank you
for your unconditional love toward us
that while we are broken by sin,
you show us what marriage can be.
May we breathe your grace, in and out,
every moment and every day.
Amen.

Two

HIS

What guy doesn't like having the remote control? You can sit back, kick up your feet, and click to whatever TV or streaming channel you want. Maybe you even think to yourself, *Relax—you've got the control.*

But it's an illusion.

For decades, glowing screens across America have been telling us as men who we're supposed to be. And we don't have control. We have confusion.

In the 1950s, we met Ward Cleaver and his lovely wife, June, on *Leave It to Beaver.* Ward showed us what it meant to be a man. He was a good provider. He was a loving father. Plus, Ward was a fellow who had all the answers—or so it seemed at the time.

In the 1970s, we met another husband and father on *All in the Family*. His name was Archie Bunker. He presented a completely different picture of manhood: lazy and always annoyed by his wife and kids.

When we changed the channel in the 1980s, a guy named Al Bundy made it clear that being *Married with Children* means that your wife and kids exist to serve you. And when they fail to do so, you make jokes at their expense.

Fast forward to the 2000s, the *Modern Family* era, which parades manliness in many forms. It's as if Al Bundy has come back as Jay, an older divorced man who's gotten remarried to a younger, more attractive wife. And there's Phil, a middle-aged husband and dad, who's made out to be a moron. Then there are Mitchell and Cameron, two gay men raising a daughter together.

If that's what the remote control has gotten us, our definition of manhood leaves a lot to be desired. Yet if we take our identity seriously as men of God, we can't just sit back, kick up our feet, relax, and surf channels until we find something that looks good.

We must take an active role in becoming the men we are created and called to be. Only then can we hope to experience the kind of marriage and family relationships God designed for men and women.

Now, you may be one of a number of people reading this:

A single guy who hopes to be married someday.
A newlywed groom who's figuring out life as a husband.
A divorced man who wishes things had gone differently.
Or a married man who wants to build a lasting legacy.

You might be the wife, mother, daughter, or sister of one of the guys mentioned above. Or you might be a single woman who's dating or looking for a man.

There's something here for all of you to apply to life—whether for your own growth, or in support of someone you care about.

In this chapter, we will be talking to men. Then in the next chapter, women, it's your turn. Now, as a quick reference, both being from the South, when speaking of men and women we like to say *fellas* and *ladies*. No matter which you are, it's important for all of us to understand our Creator's design for men and women so that we can relate to each other as he intended.

His

• • •

In the last chapter, we reviewed some statistics about the brokenness of marriage and family life today. With 12 million households parented by single moms, and 17 million children growing up without dads, that means an awful lot of young men and women don't have a clear picture of biblical manhood.

Even in traditional two-parent households, there's likely to be misunderstanding if what we watch on TV provides any reflection or influence on how we define the role of husband and father. TV is a mirror of our culture, not necessarily of biblical values.

To get a clear picture of what it means to be a man in God's eyes, we've got to do more than just change the channel. We've got to turn off the TV and go back to the original script written by our Creator.

What we discover together in God's Word is a much different story from what Ward, Archie, Al, and all the other leading men have shown us. It may also be different from the role models in our lives—our own dads, grandfathers, uncles, and brothers—depending on what kind of family we grew up in. So, for the moment, fellas, let's set all that aside and examine how the Bible defines a real man.

The Man in the Mirror

Men, take a good look in the mirror. What you see is a reflection of the image of God. And to the ladies reading this, the same is true for you. God created us in his own image, male and female, equal in dignity and value, with distinct roles for our marriage and family relationships. From the very beginning, we see within the creation narrative that God places Adam as the head or leader of his home. His role in the home is not a matter of value, but of order. It is not about authority but servant leadership.

But since sin entered the world, we also see some of Adam and

Eve's broken reflection in ours. Remember the Fall, back in the garden of Eden? God said not to eat fruit from the forbidden tree. Then the serpent showed up and tempted Eve. In Genesis 3:6, here's how the scene played out:

> **So when the woman saw that the tree was good for food, and that it was a delight to the eyes, and that the tree was to be desired to make one wise, she took of its fruit and ate, and she also gave some to her husband who was with her, and he ate.**

And here's what happened next in verses 9 to 12:

> **But the Lord God called to the man . . . "Have you eaten of the tree of which I commanded you not to eat?" The man said, "The woman whom you gave to be with me, she gave me fruit of the tree, and I ate."**

So who took the first bite?
Eve.
But whom does God hold accountable?
Adam.

And Adam is dumb, bless his heart. He tries his best to make sure God knows exactly how everything happened. You can almost hear Adam explaining, "Look, God. I was just hanging out, waiting for *SportsCenter*. Meanwhile, my wife showed up and gave me some fruit, and I ate it. So the way I see it, this is between you and her."

In Adam's mind, Eve was the one who messed up. And it's true that Eve is responsible for her actions. She sinned by eating the forbidden fruit.

But God came looking for Adam because God had put Adam in charge of Eden, before Eve was even on the scene. Rewind to Genesis 2:15 to 17:

The LORD God took the man and put him in the garden of Eden to work it and keep it. And the LORD God commanded the man, saying, "You may surely eat of every tree of the garden, but of the tree of the knowledge of good and evil you shall not eat, for in the day that you eat of it you shall surely die."

Like Eve, Adam sinned by eating the fruit. But Adam also sinned by choosing not to lead in the responsibility entrusted to him. So, God held him accountable.

Todd: The Buck Stops with Me

One year when I filed our income taxes, there was an error, so I had to re-file. If you've ever had to do that, it's a headache. I went to a tax office and re-filed the papers just like I was told. Then a few weeks later, I got a certified letter from one of my great-uncles, Sam. Some of y'all may know him. He's my crazy uncle. We don't talk about him much.

The letter basically said, *You're in trouble. You didn't give us all of the information we require, so you're going to pay a penalty.*

Here's the problem. I did everything expected of *me*, but the *tax office* failed to file a form that was needed. The tax office was responsible for the problem. But guess where the buck stops? With me.

Men, this is the principle of your *headship* in the home. It's important to recognize this God-given responsibility.

Yes, Adam and Eve *both* sinned, but they suffered different consequences. You and your wife are broken together, as we explored in the previous chapter. But based on the sin of Adam and Eve, you will experience "his" and "hers" consequences of sin. So husbands, when there is sin within the home, headship means you are held accountable.

• • •

Let's turn again to the New Testament, where Paul writes about the mystery of marriage to illustrate the gospel in the home. In Ephesians 5:22 to 24, we read,

> **Wives, submit to your own husbands, as to the Lord. For the husband is the head of the wife even as Christ is the head of the church, his body, and is himself its Savior. Now as the church submits to Christ, so also wives should submit in everything to their husbands.**

Here again we see headship. We find specifically in this text that husbands have been given this role and responsibility in the home.

Now listen, men. If this idea of headship excites you by giving you a feeling of control, then clearly the accountability we just talked about has not sunk in yet. And women, if the idea offends you, let me remind you: Headship is not about the value of being male or female, but about order. It's not about authority but about following the example of Christ, the head of the church.

We've already stated that God created men and women equal in dignity and value. Unfortunately, we're also equal in our sin and brokenness. And here's the beautiful part: In Jesus Christ, men and women share equally in grace, equally in the gospel, and equally in receiving the inheritance that is ours as sons and daughters of God.

So, look in the mirror one more time. Not only will you see a reflection of the image of God, broken by sin, but also the likeness of Christ as you become more of the man or woman he made you to be.

The Example of Christ-like Headship

When it comes to headship in the home, men tend to have three primary responses. Some *refuse* it, and some *abuse* it. But wise men *choose* to follow the example of Christ-like headship.

1. Some men refuse the responsibility of headship. We've already seen how Adam refused the responsibility God had given him. He allowed Eve to be deceived by the serpent while he sat back and watched it happen. Adam didn't step up.

Some guys just won't step up when it's time to lead. Others are lazy and entitled and don't want to put in the work required to be spiritual leaders. They behave like children rather than becoming men of God who take responsibility seriously. But 1 Corinthians 13:11 says, "When I was a child, I spoke like a child, I thought like a child, I reasoned like a child. When I became a man, I gave up childish ways." So step up from boyhood to manhood.

Other men are just irresponsible. They would rather pass off their responsibility on somebody else. They give it to the school system, their kids' coaches, their wives, anybody. These men don't want to be the head of the home. And it's a problem.

2. Some men abuse the position of headship. No doubt, men like this have affected many of us. They're oppressive and domineering, strong-handed and cold-hearted. Rather than leading out of love, they dominate out of fear.

Guys, whether you're married or not, you need to know that God has called us to be leaders, not authoritarians. Just because people do what you want doesn't mean you're a leader.

Pastor Darrin Patrick says men are typically defined in one of two ways:[9] They're either *out* of control or they try to be *in* control all the

---

9. Darrin Patrick, *The Dude's Guide to Manhood* (Nashville, TN: Thomas Nelson, 2014).

time. Either extreme misses what biblical headship is meant to be. Someone can abuse authority as a businessman, a boss, a coach, or a dad. And there's a saying: "Authority is like a bar of soap. The more you use, the less you have."[10]

Todd: A Repair Man vs. A Prayer Man

A while back, Adrian was struggling with a decision, so she came and said, "Hey, I've got this problem . . ."

Immediately, I went into defensive husband mode. I wanted to fix the problem. I wanted to repair the issue. I was thinking, *You have a problem? I have an answer. Let's do these three things. Bam! Problem solved, conversation ended.*

During the conversation, my wife said, "Maybe we should pray about this and see what the Lord wants us to do."

But I just kept talking. "We need to do this and that and blah, blah, blah." I never prayed with her. I just wanted to fix the problem.

Except she didn't need a repair man. She needed a prayer man.

The next day the Holy Spirit was all over me about it.

So I approached Adrian and picked up the conversation again. "Listen," I said. "I failed you yesterday, and I want you to know that I'm sorry. Forgive me. I reacted and tried to fix the problem without taking it to the Lord." So I put my arms around her, and we prayed about it then and there.

---

10. Quotation originates with John Richard Wimber

3. Wise men *choose* the example of Christ-like headship. Don't *refuse*, don't *abuse*, but rather *choose* the example of Jesus Christ. In Ephesians 5:25 to 30, Paul described this example for us:

> Husbands, love your wives, as Christ loved the church and gave himself up for her, that he might sanctify her, having cleansed her by the washing of water with the word, so that he might present the church to himself in splendor, without spot or wrinkle or any such thing, that she might be holy and without blemish. In the same way husbands should love their wives as their own bodies. He who loves his wife loves himself. For no one ever hated his own flesh, but nourishes and cherishes it, just as Christ does the church, because we are members of his body.

With each command to husbands, did you notice how Christ is the supreme example? We might have expected this passage to say, "Wives, submit to your husbands because he's the head of the home; and husbands, rule over your wives."

But that's not what it says.

Why?

Because leadership is about loving those who have been entrusted to you. And when we model our leadership after the headship of Christ, we see the glory of the gospel in the home.

Pastor Eric Mason, author of *Manhood Restored*, writes about the responsibility of Christ-like headship: "Jesus is the prototype man for men. All of us men are only as manly as it relates to the standard set by Jesus."[11]

With this in mind, let's take a closer look at real manhood.

---

11. Eric Mason, *Manhood Restored* (Nashville, TN: B&H Publishers, 2013), 45.

Real manhood is marked by supernatural love.

We just read from Ephesians 5:25, "Husbands, love your wives *as Christ loved* the church." That's a high standard for real manhood. Because the example of love we see in Christ—that's supernatural love. And by ourselves, men, we know deep down that we're inadequate to live up to that standard.

You might be a guy whose life is *out* of control. Think about it.
How's your language?
Your finances?
Your work?
Anger?
Alcohol?
Maybe even pornography?
Are you out of control in any of these areas?

Or you might be trying too hard to keep things *in* control. You keep a tight grip on everything. It's your way or the highway. You may be frustrated and thinking, *I'm doing absolutely everything I know to do.*
The truth is, you can't pull yourself up by your bootstraps to achieve the real manhood we're talking about. That's where the gospel comes in.

You can be rescued from a life that is running *out* of control.
You can be released from a life of striving to be *in* control.
And you can be redeemed *for* a life of thriving *under* control.

We thrive as men who are under control when we live in submission to the power of the Holy Spirit in our lives. The context of Ephesians 5:25 goes back to a command given to us in verse 18, which says, "Do not get drunk with wine, for that is debauchery, but *be filled with the Spirit.*" Paul's directive for both men and women in regards to their role in the home is only possible through the "filling" of the Holy

Spirit. We are unable in our own power to lead in a supernatural love. So what do we do? We tap into that power when we accept that Jesus Christ has made a way to redeem us from sin. Jesus is our supreme example of supernatural love, our supreme example of real manhood, and the Holy Spirit is then our source of power that enables us to love like him.

Real manhood is marked by a sacrificial love.

We're not finished yet with Ephesians 5:25. It says, "Husbands, love your wives, as Christ loved the church and *gave himself up* for her." Jesus Christ died for the church. He went to the cross. He gave his life as a sacrifice to pay the full penalty for the forgiveness of sin, so that we could be redeemed.

He didn't pay 10 percent.
He didn't pay 80 percent.
He didn't pay 98 percent.
Jesus paid it all.

He loved us before we ever loved him.
He offered us forgiveness before we even knew to ask for it.
He made the first move to restore our broken relationship.
Jesus did this for us.

Talk about real manhood.

When our lives are marked by sacrificial love, our leadership will bring harmony in the home. We'll be the first ones giving our all, showing love, initiating forgiveness, and seeking restoration—not waiting for someone else to step up. With servant leadership like that, just imagine how our marriage and family life can illustrate the radical grace of God. What a beautiful portrait of the gospel in the home.

Now, let's put this into practical terms. The sacrificial love of Jesus Christ is not just relational; it's physical. He literally died for us.

So men, we have to be willing to give our lives.

You're thinking, *I would take a bullet for my wife.* And you mean it. Hopefully, it won't ever come to that.

But how about serving her in simple ways? Taking out the trash. Tackling the honey-do list. Enjoying a date night. Staying home with the kids while she goes out with her girlfriends. Or if money is tight, giving up what you spend on your hobby.

Whether in the ultimate sacrifice or in much smaller ones, real manhood is being willing to give it all.

Real manhood is marked by sanctifying love.

As we keep reading in Ephesians 5, we can learn even more from the example of Christ's love for the church. Here again is verse 26 to 27:

> That he might sanctify her, having cleansed her by the washing of water with the word, so that he might present the church to himself in splendor, without spot or wrinkle or any such thing, that she might be holy and without blemish.

This imagery refers to the Jewish ritual of preparing a bride for her wedding day. According to New Testament scholar, Craig Keener:

> After this washing the bride was perfumed, anointed, and arrayed in wedding clothes. The betrothal ceremony in Judaism also came to be called "the sanctification of the bride," setting her apart for her husband.[12]

---

12. Craig Keener, The IVP Bible Background Commentary: New Testament, (Downers Grove, IL: IVP Academic, 1993), 552.

Christ not only sacrificed his life to redeem his bride, the church, but he also wants to sanctify the church. To *sanctify* means to set apart. So that when Christ returns, the church will be spotless, without wrinkle or blemish.

It sounds like what your wife would call a makeover—except this one goes way more than skin deep. It goes to the heart. Christ is refining the character of the church, making his bride beautiful, preparing her for eternity with him.

Husbands, your responsibility in the home is to follow this example of sanctifying love in relationship with your wife. Through you, God seeks to refine her character and bring out her beauty. So ask yourself, *Is she growing in love for Christ? Is she worshiping God with all her heart? Are her gifts being discovered, valued, and used?*

To answer these questions for her, you have to ask the same things of yourself. Your leadership in spiritual life at home requires that you pursue godliness in your *own* life. It's more than skin deep for you too. You've got to be growing as an authentic man who has a heart for Christ.

You can't let sin go unchecked. Not in the way you talk to your wife. Not in workaholic habits. Not in personal integrity. Not in sexual impurity. You will never be able to see your family grow in sanctification without pursuing godliness yourself.

This means becoming a man of prayer, seeking the power of the Holy Spirit in your life. Pray privately. Pray with and for your family.

This means becoming a man of God's Word, studying to know what it says and how to live it out. You might have to get up early or stay up late to spend more time in the pages of Scripture. Or you might join a men's Bible study so you can learn with and from others.

A word of warning is needed here. Because some men tend to think, *I don't know the Bible as well as my wife does, so I'll let her lead in this area at home.*

Wrong answer.

You can't pass off this responsibility if you're going to be a real man who leads with sanctifying love. Let your wife see your relationship with God in prayer. Let your family see how your decisions are based on the principles of God's Word.

Christ is not an accessory. He's not an app on your phone that you click only when you need it. He's your operating system. He's at the very center of your life, your marriage, and your family—all being sanctified, set apart for him.

Connor: The Importance of Spiritual Huddles at Home

Mary and I are 16 years in. We've been praying together since we were engaged, and there are still times when it's awkward. So if you feel a bit embarrassed, be okay with that. Don't let it keep you from praying with and for your wife.

Let me encourage you to grab her hand, and if you don't know what to say, just say, "Ready, set, hut!" And after a few minutes you can break the huddle with "Amen."

With Mary, I also make a point to talk about what she's reading in God's Word. I might ask, "What's the Lord teaching you?" Or, based on what I'm studying, I might ask, "What do you think this means? Are you seeing the same things I am?"

Instead of telling Mary what to do in her spiritual walk, I want to lead and encourage her discovery of what God has in store for her. And even if it's awkward sometimes, I want our home to be a place where she can seek truth and wise counsel with me.

His

Real manhood is marked by sustaining love.

Let's circle back to Ephesians 5, where verses 28 to 30 further describe the example of Christ-like love:

In the same way husbands should love their wives as their own bodies. He who loves his wife loves himself. For no one ever hated his own flesh, but nourishes and cherishes it, just as Christ does the church, because we are members of his body.

Words like *nourish* and *cherish* are not exactly macho. But listen, men, those are the very words Paul uses to describe sustaining love. It's ongoing. It's not a check box, but a commitment to a way of life. When you love your wife like that, you create a home environment where she and your children feel safe and cared for.

Most of us men need to have this spelled out in everyday terms. Moreover, here are some specific ways you can demonstrate sustaining love at home.

1. Provide financially. Take responsibility for the finances in your household. This doesn't mean you make all the money or write all the checks. It means you lead. Develop a budget. Create a spending plan. Make sure there's money going into the savings account.

It also means that you make plans to sustain your family if something happens to you. Get an insurance policy. Plan ahead to ensure a solid financial future.

2. Protect physically and spiritually. You know what it means to be the physical protector of your home. For sure, if something goes *bump* in the night, you're the one who gets up to check it out. But the protection of sustaining love isn't about only physical safety. You protect your wife by not letting anyone tear her down, by not letting anyone speak disrespectfully of her or to her. *Ever.*

As for your family, God has placed you like a watchman on the wall. You need to know whom your children are hanging out with, whom they're dating. You need to be familiar with what's happening in the social media world they live in.

You're also the spiritual protector of your home. That means you're praying for your wife and children. That means you don't passively sit back and watch any of them drift away from the Lord, just hoping they'll turn around. No, you step up as a spiritual leader, and you do so with gentleness and love.

3. Connect emotionally. Guys, this is a challenging assignment for us. Consider what 1 Peter 3:7 says:

> **Likewise, husbands, live with your wives in an understanding way, showing honor to the woman as the weaker vessel, since they are heirs with you of the grace of life, so that your prayers may not be hindered.**

This verse contains deep wisdom to draw from. First of all, to live with your wife *in an understanding way* means you have intimate knowledge of her. Study her. Find out what makes her tick. Pay attention to how she changes with the seasons of life.

What are her passions?
What are her gifts?
How can you help her thrive?
What does "I love you" mean for her? Not for you.

Speaking of what love means for her, let's get something out in the open. When you express emotional connection with physical touch, you're often thinking about sex—probably more often than not. But she needs to know that holding your hand, exchanging a kiss, or feeling your arms around her is not attached only to an expectation of sex. Otherwise, she will resent your affection as a ploy for your satisfaction, not hers.

....

Connor: From Date Days to Diapers

When Mary and I were newlyweds, we would have date days. On Saturday we would get up, have breakfast, and then go out shopping or horsing around for a while. Then we'd see an afternoon movie. Then dinner. Then maybe rent a movie to watch at home that night.

It sounds crazy, I know. But we had no children and a dual income. So I could say "I love you" to Mary in all these ways. But sixteen years and five children later, do you know what Mary wants?

"Connor, could you keep the kids while I go to the grocery store by myself?"

We have three kids in diapers. Mary tells me one of the times she finds me most sexy is when I'm changing diapers. So, guess what I'm doing often?

"Oh, dang! I think they're wet."

"No, they're not. I just changed them."

"Oh, I'm not so sure." You know what I mean?

....

When you were reading that last verse in 1 Peter, did you wonder what it meant about *showing honor to the woman as the weaker vessel?* Too many times this phrase has been misunderstood as demeaning or sexist. But in the Greek language of the New Testament, it's the strongest expression of respect.

In the first-century Roman world, women were considered the property of men, with no rights, no education, and no role in society except childbearing. So it was counter-cultural to show honor to a woman. What a crazy idea—like comparing a Dixie cup to fine china. Your wife is not disposable; she's a family heirloom. An heirloom means something not because of what it's worth financially but because of what it's worth emotionally. You can't put a price tag on it.

And the verse goes on: *since they are heirs with you of the grace of life.* What this means is that, before she is your wife, she is God's daughter. The Creator God of the universe has entrusted you with something infinitely valuable to *him,* not to mention her significance to you. So you'd better treat her with great care.

There are spiritual implications to the next phrase: *so that your prayers may not be hindered.* Your love relationship with your wife will directly reflect your relationship with God.

So cherish the woman he has entrusted to you. Respect her. Brag on her in front of your children. Speak well of her to your friends. When you do, you'll create more than an emotional connection with her—you'll build a home marked by sustaining love.

• • •

Some people have a little plaque on their wall that says, "As for me and my house, we will serve the Lord." It might look so quaint that you'd never guess the powerful story it comes from—a great story of real manhood.

The Old Testament book of Joshua tells how God delivers the people of Israel from slavery in Egypt and brings them into the Promised Land. But did you know that the Promised Land was occupied territory? So, the Israelites had to drive out the occupants of Canaan. They engage in battle after battle after battle. It's a bloody, dirty, messy way for the Israelites to begin their life in the Promised Land.

In the midst of all this, some of the people of Israel begin to worship false gods of the Canaanites. Others begin to worship some of the gods of Egypt. And still others give up worshiping at all.

But among the Israelites there's a man of God named Joshua, a fearless leader. He calls all the men of Israel together for a giant huddle. In Joshua 24:15, he gives one of the best locker room speeches ever recorded:

> **And if it is evil in your eyes to serve the LORD, choose this day whom you will serve, whether the gods your fathers served in the region beyond the River, or the gods of the Amorites in whose land you dwell. But as for me and my house, we will serve the LORD.**

Men, this is a battle cry for us. God is saying to us, "If you want to fulfill the very role and calling I have given you, then choose this day whom you will serve."

How will you respond to the call?
It's your choice.

Will you serve the God who has radically rescued and saved you?
Will you live under the control of the Holy Spirit who empowers you?
It's your choice.

You might be thinking, *No, you don't know how I was raised.* But this isn't about your father or the chances you didn't have. It's about following the example of Christ.
It's your choice.

You might be thinking, *She's about to leave. She's already gone. It's over.* Maybe so. But from this day forward, only you can determine the kind of man you will become.
It's your choice.

Gospel in the Home

Only you can echo the words of Joshua:
"But as for me and my house, we will serve the Lord."

We have become confused by cultural messages about manhood. But the biblical call is clear. In the home, men are called to lead by example—the example of Christ in supernatural, sacrificial, sanctifying, and sustaining love. When we accept this role and responsibility, we live out the grace of the gospel in the home.

Lord Jesus Christ,
May we as husbands and brothers,
fathers and sons,
seek after you with all of our hearts
so that we may become the men you made us to be.
We choose this day to serve you.
Amen.

Three
HERS

You can tell a lot about a woman by going shopping with her. We've all heard jokes about this—and to the ladies who are reading this, we promise we're laughing *with* you, not *at* you. Really. Because when a guy is shopping for golf or hunting gear . . . well, you know how it goes.

Recently, there's been a story circulating online about a new kind of store. It's a place where women can choose a husband from among various kinds of men. The store has many floors, and as the shopper goes up from one to the next, she finds available men with increasingly positive attributes.

But there's a catch.

Once she upgrades to the next floor, she can't go back down to shop again on a lower floor; either she chooses a husband, or she exits the building.

One day, a woman goes into the store. She can hardly wait to discover what fine specimens are on display. As she enters, she sees a sign.

Floor One: These men have jobs.

The woman says to herself, "That's better than my last boyfriend, but I wonder what's on the next floor." So she takes the elevator to the second floor. The doors open.

Floor Two: These men have jobs and they love kids.

She pauses. "Hmmm, that's pretty good." But she's curious about what she might be missing on the next floor, so she stays on the elevator.

Floor Three: These men have jobs, they love kids, and they're extremely good-looking.

Pretty good just got better. "Maybe just one more floor," she thinks.

Floor Four: These men have jobs, they love kids, they're extremely good-looking, and they help with housework.

"Wow. Very tempting." But she presses the next button, and up she goes.

Floor Five: These men have jobs, they love kids, they're extremely good-looking, they help with housework, and they have a strong romantic streak.

"Oh my goodness. Can it get any better than this? There's only one way to find out." The woman heads to the sixth floor with great anticipation. She can't wait to choose an amazing husband.

Floor Six: You are visitor number 3,456,789,012. There are no men on this floor. This floor exists solely as proof that women are impossible to please. Thanks for shopping at HusbandMart, and have a nice day.

Guys, the owner of the store has just opened up a wives store where you can shop directly across the street. The first floor has wives who love sex. The second floor has wives who love sex and have money. Floors three through six have never been visited.

All joking aside, this chapter is not about finding the perfect husband or, for that matter, the perfect wife. There is no such thing, and we all know it. We are broken. When it comes to marriage, as we've said before, we often try to ride the bicycle backwards, contrary to its design. But we have begun to see how God desires to redeem men and women to create a beautiful portrait of the gospel in the home.

The last chapter had something for everyone, and this one does too. We will be speaking especially to women, but we know men are listening in. So, whether you come from a "his" or "hers" perspective, and whether you are single, married, or divorced, we hope you will gain greater understanding of God's design for marriage and for the fullness of life he created.

You already know that we are fellas from the South, where we were brought up to respect ladies. We don't claim to know what it's like to walk in women's shoes—either literally or figuratively—but we will do our best to communicate what God's Word says for you. And, we are thankful for our wives and daughters who give us the opportunity to see how they grow in Christ-likeness every day.

• • •

Just as our image of manhood is distorted by what we see on TV, so is the picture of womanhood in our culture today. Stereotypes of women often represent two extremes. One is weak and helpless like the classic damsel in distress. The other wields sex and power like the so-called *Real Housewives* on TV.

Somewhere in the middle, a lot of women are trying to figure out who they really are—who God made and called them to be. It can be a scary place for women themselves, and for moms and dads trying to raise daughters and sons who respect real womanhood. How can you respect what you don't even know?

Without knowing who they were meant to be, women struggle to find satisfaction as they live with the consequences of brokenness in our culture and in their own choices. And, sadly, many women are abused, mistreated and degraded.

Like men, women can't remedy their brokenness by living *out* of control or trying to be *in* control. So we're going to look at how the gospel redeems women to live *under* the control of the Holy Spirit. The fruit of the Spirit includes self-control, which is an important trait of real womanhood.

The Woman in the Mirror

You know the fairytale question: *Mirror, mirror on the wall, who's the fairest of them all?* It echoes the real-life pressure women feel to measure up to standards of external beauty.

Yet, the beauty of real womanhood begins with understanding that you were made in the image of God, the *Imago Dei*, as we learned from the story of Adam and Eve. And tragically, our reflection of his image has been broken by sin.

But hear this: The gospel restores beauty where brokenness has left its deepest scars in a woman's soul. In a biblical view, real womanhood gives attention to *internal* and *eternal* beauty. Look at what 1 Peter 3:3 to 4 says:

> **Do not let your adorning be external—the braiding of hair and the putting on of gold jewelry, or the clothing you wear—but let your adorning be the hidden person of the heart with the imperishable beauty of a gentle and quiet spirit, which in God's sight is very precious.**

Women, you don't have to find your identity in how you look. This doesn't mean it's wrong to have an attractive appearance. But understand that external things—whether your clothes, your house, or your career—reveal what's important in your heart. So we are going to examine the heart of real womanhood.

Proverbs 31:30 says it another way: "Charm is deceitful, and beauty is vain, but a woman who fears the Lord is to be praised." There's nothing more attractive in your wardrobe than godliness. It shows in how you carry yourself. People think, *What a beautiful woman.* And a husband feels like the most blessed man in the world to have a wife like that.

Other verses in Proverbs show us the opposite picture. It's a bit humorous and frightening at the same time. Proverbs 21 says in verse 9, "It is better to live in a corner of the housetop than in a house shared with a quarrelsome wife." And in verse 19, "It is better to live in a desert land than with a quarrelsome and fretful woman." *Ouch.*

Then, in Proverbs 27:15 we find this verse: "A continual dripping on a rainy day and a quarrelsome wife are alike." Ladies, no amount of external beauty can make up for a leaky-faucet personality that goes drip . . . drip . . . drip . . . and drives a husband crazy.

As much as your husband doesn't want to live that way, we're pretty sure you don't either. So, from this day forward, you are invited to fully embrace your calling as a woman of God—a calling that will develop your timeless beauty from the inside out.

....

Todd: The power of a godly wife

I'm telling you, I'm married to the most amazing woman. I say this in all humility. My wife is not perfect. She's growing in Christ, just like any other person. She would want me to say that. But I'm telling you from personal experience what an absolute joy it is to live with and lead a woman who walks in Christlikeness. It is an absolute pleasure to be married to her. This year, Adrian and I are celebrating our 15th wedding anniversary and I can tell you that our marriage has never been better. However, the first few years had their sketchy moments. Not to say it was all bad, but in all honesty, I had a lot to learn about what it meant to be a husband and leader. I would describe myself in the early years as selfish, inconsiderate, and very self-absorbed. What changed? Well, obviously the changes I've made have been a work of the Holy Spirit in my life. At the same time, I have to say that Adrian has played a big part in my spiritual maturity. Her patience, selflessness, and Christ-like humility have allowed me to grow. Rather than nagging me to death over inadequacies, constantly beating me down when I fail, or passively ignoring weaknesses, she encourages and builds me up daily. She is my biggest fan. Her willingness to lovingly and patiently communicate the areas in which I need to grow and her example of a selfless, Christ-like spirit have made all of the difference in my life. While I still have a lot to learn, I am absolutely a different man because of the way God has used her in my life. This is the power of a godly woman in the life of her husband.

....

We will be looking closely at Titus 2:3 to 5 as we explore what real womanhood looks like.

Older women likewise are to be reverent in behavior, not slanderers or slaves to much wine. They are to teach what is good, and so train the young women to love their husbands and children, to be self-controlled, pure, working at home, kind, and submissive to their own husbands, that the word of God may not be reviled.

By the way, that word *older* is not necessarily about age, but rather maturity. A woman of God is to be maturing in faith and growing in grace as she follows Christ. In time, maturity gives you a platform to *teach what is good* to younger women. This is not a right that comes with age; it's a responsibility that comes with maturity. It's a response to the call of Christ to "make disciples."

So, whether you are older or younger, who are you discipling? And who is discipling you? In what relationships are you giving and receiving encouragement to grow in God's grace and live it out in daily life?

As you seek to develop in your experience of real womanhood, let's consider what Scripture reveals for you.

Real womanhood is marked by the pursuit of holiness.

Women, let us say here the same thing we said to men. On your own, you are inadequate to fulfill the role God has entrusted to you. But the grace of God, through Jesus Christ, can redeem you and enable you. Those verses from Titus are not a checklist of things for you to do to become a better woman. Rather, they describe how the gospel reshapes your life to produce holiness you could never achieve as a matter of self-effort.

Bible Study writer Josh Hunt puts it this way: "The lifestyle of godliness is both the logical consequence and living result of the good news of forgiveness and new life in Christ being accepted into our hearts."[13]

And by the way, no other person who has ever lived has done more for the cause of women's rights than Jesus Christ. If you look at women in the first-century Roman world, and then you compare how the gospel has transformed the way they are treated, you will see that Jesus was and is an advocate for women. He gave his life to prove that

---

13. Josh Hunt, *Good Questions Have Small Groups Talking,* www.joshhunt.com, Titus, Lesson #2, question 5, line 4 and following. Notes for May 19, 2013.

he loves you. He wants to sanctify you, to set you apart for himself by refining your character and bringing out your true beauty.

You might be wondering, *What does that look like in practical terms?* Well, let's highlight three specific things.

1. Serve reverently in the church. Look again at Titus 2:3, which says, "Older women likewise are to be *reverent in behavior.* This specifically refers to behavior in the temple, God's church. For a woman of God, the church is not an afterthought, it's a priority. It's not a social gathering, it's a community of believers committed to God's Word. As 1 Peter 2:9 says, "You [believers] are a chosen race, a royal priesthood," which simply means we are servants of the living God. As you serve him in and through the church, a reverent spirit is a mark of holiness.

2. Express love in your speech. Titus 2:3 also says that older women are not to be *slanderers.* The word *slander* means to make a false statement about a person, which damages their character.

> Have you ever torn down a girlfriend's character with your words?
> Have you ever made light of a coworker's failure or weakness?
> Have you ever posted catty comments on social media?
> Have you ever shared a so-called "prayer request" that was really an excuse to gossip?
> Have you ever rolled your eyes to imply that your husband just doesn't get it?

These choices miss the mark of holiness defined in 1 Corinthians 13:6: Love "does not rejoice at wrongdoing but rejoices with the truth."

3. Show moderation in your lifestyle. The passage in Titus warns us not to be *slaves to much wine.* The issue here is indulgence where restraint would be the wiser choice—and yes, it's as true for men as for women.

But speaking to women, if you get together socially and can't do so without alcohol, you may not have an alcohol problem; but you may well have an identity problem. Alcohol can be used to mask anxiety and insecurity, one glass of wine at a time.

Consumption of alcohol is not predominately a sin issue but a wisdom issue. Let's be honest: Many people can't handle it, so wisdom says many should abstain. As the saying goes, "Just because you can doesn't mean you should."

Now, maybe you're thinking, *alcohol is not a problem for me*. So, think about your other lifestyle choices. How are you doing with food? Or social media? Or TV? Or spending? In all things, holiness produces moderation.

Here's the bottom line: Holiness allows us to enjoy the gifts of God without making gods of those gifts. So, as a woman pursues holiness, those around her will see evidence in reverent service, in loving speech, and in a lifestyle of moderation.

Real womanhood is marked by the presence of Christ-like character.

Let's return to Titus 2, and this time look at verses 4 to 5: "Train the young women to love their husbands and children, to be self-controlled, pure." Every word here is significant. We will look at them one by one so you can discover the presence of Christ-like character in this description of womanhood.

First, the word *train* reminds us that it's not always natural to do what this verse says. Titus was a young pastor of a congregation full of sinners. It's the same with every pastor and every church. And because we're all sinners, our nature doesn't always bend itself toward godliness. [In fact, Augustine said that our lack of godliness means that we are bent inward on ourselves, rather than outward toward

God and others.] We need to be trained to know and practice Christlike character. Think of a sapling tree—it needs support to grow upright.

The training of younger women is specific: *to love their husbands and children*, then *to be self-controlled* and *pure*. Consider the practical application to your life and marriage.

1. Love your husband. The word *love* here is not some mystical, emotional force. It's not an unstoppable romantic feeling that sweeps over you. Rather, this biblical word for love is rooted in resolve. The literal meaning is to *be loving*, with an emphasis on behavior. Show your husband how much you value him—as if you'd taken the elevator all the way up to the 100th floor to find him.

So how can you practically express love to your husband?

Study him.
Support him.
Serve him.

If you read a book on how to love your spouse, you're going to discover how to love the author's spouse. So, ladies, when it comes to loving *your* man, study him. Figure out what makes him tick and what "I love you" means for him.

Then also support him. Your husband needs to know that you're in his corner no matter what—that your love for him is unconditional like that of Jesus. Let him know he has a safe place to take risks, even if he sometimes fails. When he knows he has your full support, not second-guessing, it's jet fuel to his soul.

Finally, serve your husband. Your guy is blessed when you pay attention to his spiritual, emotional, and physical needs. Pray for him. Encourage him. When he's flying with blinders on, be his lookout. And don't neglect God's gift of sex to be enjoyed in your marriage; show him you love him that way too.

Hers

Connor: A Love Letter of Support

Not long after we got married, Mary and I liquidated our savings to start a landscape business in Dallas. I had gone to school at Texas Tech for a degree in landscape architecture, and that's what I wanted to do for the rest of my life. You can see how that turned out. Now I live in Longview and pastor a church.

Well, the business grew very quickly, and a much larger company offered to buy it and hire me to run the operations. At the same time, we had just had our first baby. So there was a lot for us to pray about. *Was it the right career move? Was it the best thing for our family?*

I'll never forget a note I received from Mary as we were considering what to do. She wrote,

Connor, I know that things are stressful right now, but God is in control. You're a wonderful husband and provider, and I am not worried about how all this will work out . . .

You remember when we started this company we anchored it on this verse, Isaiah 43:19: "Behold, I am doing a new thing; now it springs forth, do you not perceive it? I will make a way in the wilderness and rivers in the desert."

I love you very much. I just want this to be a prayerful and well-thought-out decision. We have to feel confident in our decision. I love you and support you either way.

Nothing she has ever done in our lives together has meant more to me than her encouragement and support. My wife will be the first to tell you she's not perfect, but she's growing in Christ-like character. I see it in the way she supports me.

She responded the same way when I felt that God was calling me to sell that lucrative business and go into ministry. She said, "I've got your back. Whatever that looks like, I'm in."

2. Love your children. It's not by accident that Titus 2:4 says for women to love their husbands, then their children. This is the order God designed, although it doesn't always happen that way for everyone—and when it doesn't, the grace of God abounds for you. God has given wives who become mothers a capacity for both roles, but not the role of mother at the expense of the role of wife.

As a wife, one of the greatest gifts you can give your husband is the absolute affirmation that you love his children, but you are devoted first to him. This is also one of the greatest gifts you can give your children, so they can see a mom who loves their dad.

Your children need to know you love them too. But beware that in our culture, many parents—moms and dads alike—have come to view their children as obstacles to avoid or idols to worship. On the one hand, we may fear that children will get in the way of experiencing all of the opportunities and joys of life; when that happens in our culture, the result may be abortion, neglect, or abuse. On the other hand, we may make our children the very center of our identity; when that happens, we spoil them or hold them to idealistic standards of achievement so *we* feel fulfilled. If you make your children your idols, they will be crushed under the weight of your expectations.

Godly women do not see their children as obstacles or idols, but as blessings from God to be loved, nurtured, and protected in the love of Christ. Moms, do you know this? Your kids are on loan from God. Take great joy in loving them.

Connor: A Bundle of Unexpected Joy

When Mary got pregnant with the youngest of our five children, it was a surprise. We had thought our family was complete.

But here's the thing. Of our five children, the third and

fourth don't speak or walk because of some severe health conditions they were born with. So all of the things we took for granted with the oldest two kids, we then missed desperately with the next two. Now, with the addition of a fifth, God is graciously allowing us joy I never knew I'd have again.

Moms, can I tell you what I've learned from this? Look for God's grace in your kids. Find it, and then seek to instill it in them. Encourage them in the love of Jesus, and teach them the gospel of Jesus. This is what it means to love your children.

....

3. Be self-controlled. Titus 2:5 also says to *be self-controlled*. Remember what we said earlier about not living *out* of control or trying to be *in* control, but rather *under* control? The Holy Spirit empowers you to live with self-control.

It means not saying or doing the first thing that comes to mind.
It means not having to be right all of the time.
It means not telling your guy when he's wrong sometimes.
It means biting your tongue when you're tempted to complain.
It means guarding your head and your heart, so that your thoughts and your emotions reflect the love of Christ.

4. Be morally pure. There's so much in this one little word: *pure*. It relates to self-control and the internal beauty we've already talked about.

Let's be direct here: We live in a culture that's chasing the hearts of women to make unhealthy emotional and sexual connections. But don't flirt with temptation. Whether you are single or married, there is zero room in your life for movies and books like *Magic Mike* and *Fifty Shades of Grey*. They open Pandora's box. They put images in your mind and desires in your heart that God did not intend. They contaminate what God designed for pure joy.

And husbands, if you promote explicit content in your house because you like the sexual payoff, then stop it. Confess it. Take the lead. Be like Joshua—it's your choice.

Purity is godliness having its way in your heart and being made visible in your behavior.

Real womanhood is about the presence of Christ *in* you being lived *through* you. It is marked by love for your husband and children. It is marked by self-control and moral purity.

Real womanhood is marked by the priority of the home.

Let's review Titus 2:3 to 5 again, taking time to notice the words we have examined so far, as well as the next phrase we will consider: *working at home.*

> **Older women likewise are to be reverent in behavior, not slanderers or slaves to much wine. They are to teach what is good, and so train the young women to love their husbands and children, to be self-controlled, pure, working at home, kind, and submissive to their own husbands, that the word of God may not be reviled.**

In the Greek language of New Testament manuscripts, the idea here is domestic. It's saying, *See to it that the domestic responsibilities of managing your household take priority in your life.*

This is about meeting the needs of your husband and children. It doesn't mean you can't work outside the home. It doesn't mean you're the one who has to do all of the housework. Here's what it *does* mean, though: Your life at home should be your priority. Period.

We live in a culture that tells you, "*You can have it all. You can have the ideal marriage, the best kids, the perfect home, and an amazing career—everything you've ever dreamed. You don't have to sacrifice anything."*

That's not reality for any woman, or any man, for that matter. Everything that is worth something will cost you something. That's just how the world works. There are sacrifices. If you're going to put one thing first, then something else is going to take second place. Logic says you can't have it all. But what you *can* have is God's best, and God's best says your home takes priority.

Let's put it this way: If you leave your job tomorrow, you will be replaced in short order. But at home, you're it. You're the wife and mother. And here again, the same is true for the husband and father. Nobody can replace your unique, God-given roles at home.

So if your job is getting in the way of this priority, you may need to consider changing jobs. You may need to accept that your career will not take the path you had hoped when you were in school. You may have to downsize your lifestyle. You and your husband need to prayerfully consider these things for the sake of the home you are creating together.

Women, you may be wondering what it looks like to make home a priority in the context of your life. Well, why don't you take five minutes and read Proverbs 31:10 to 31. Go ahead, we'll wait for you.

This is an awesome woman.

She's an entrepreneur.
She's wheeling and dealing at the busiest market.
She's providing good food for her family.
She's creative.
She's into fashion.
She's dressing her husband and her children well.
She's compassionate toward the poor.
She's wise and respected in the community.
She's receiving praise from her husband and children.

After all she does inside and outside the home, verses 28 to 29 say,

> **Her children rise up and call her blessed;**
> **her husband also, and he praises her:**
> **"Many women have done excellently,**
> **but you surpass them all."**

What woman would not want to be honored like that? You may look at Proverbs 31 with fresh eyes today and find it inspiring. Or, you may feel like it's an impossible list of expectations you can't live up to. Either way, be assured that this passage is not a fairytale mirror to determine who's the fairest of them all.

Women, there's a bigger message for you: Hone your gifts, whatever they may be, so that your life at home can flourish as God intends. This is a mark of real womanhood.

Real womanhood is marked by the practice of submission.

By now you've already seen that hot-button word—*submissive*—in Titus 2:5. We're going to address the meaning we find in Scripture, as well as the misunderstanding we often find in our culture.

Submission has become a theological *earworm*. Do you know what that is? A song that gets stuck in your head, and you can't get it out. You can probably think of several.

> *Y-M-C-A!*
> *We . . . will . . . we . . . will . . . rock you.*
> *Vanilla . . . Ice Ice . . . Baby . . .*
> Or the all-time classic, *It's a small world after all.*

When an earworm gets stuck in your head, it annoys you regardless of whether you bother to think about what it means.

Submission.

It's been said that the best way to get rid of an earworm is to listen to the song in its entirety. Most of us know the earworm but not the whole song. So let's listen through what Paul says about submission in Ephesians 5:22 to 24.

Wives, submit to your own husbands, as to the Lord. For the husband is the head of the wife even as Christ is the head of the church, his body, and is himself its Savior. Now as the church submits to Christ, so also wives should submit in everything to their husbands.

Do you hear the love song of redemption? The Scriptures reference headship in the relationship between husband and wife as an echo of the relationship that exists between Jesus Christ and his church, his bride. In the previous chapter, we already saw how Ephesians 5:26 to 27 goes on to reference the Jewish ritual of a bride preparing for her wedding day. So imagine this love song as a wedding dance.

Ultimately, submission to your husband is about your submission to Christ. This is why verse 22 says *as to the Lord.* God has placed your husband as the head of your home as Christ is the head of the church.

When you really listen to the song of submission, it affirms a valuable truth for women and men alike. Our lives as followers of Christ are defined by submission. Every one of us is called to yield ourselves to his authority in our lives. And throughout the New Testament, we find practical instructions for believers to submit to authority because we have chosen to submit to Christ. We submit to our employers, to our government, to the leadership of our local church. Wives submit to their husbands and children to their parents. In all these ways, we practice submission.

• • •

Just as important as understanding what submission is, is understanding what it's not.

First of all, submission is not *all* women to *all* men. Notice that Ephesians 5:22 says for wives to submit to their *own* husband. This is specific to the context of *your* marriage.

Second, submission is not absolute in every situation. If a husband is abusive, if he is unfaithful and unrepentant, if he is asking you to do something immoral or illegal—you are not obligated, ladies, to submit to a man like that. Seek help from a pastor or counselor or trusted friend. Your husband needs to be held accountable to the biblical standard of real manhood.

Third, submission is not about value and worth. Men and women are both created in the image of God—equal in our value while being distinct in our roles. We saw this in Genesis 1 to 2. And, we see in Galatians 3:28 that in Christ, "There is no male and female." In the gospel, we are equal recipients of the grace of God.

• • •

We said earlier that the beauty of submission resembles a wedding dance. Maybe you've watched *Dancing with the Stars*, so you've seen how the male partner leads and the female partner follows him to the rhythm of the music. It's the only way two dance partners can keep in step with each other. And when they do it well, those of us who are watching will hardly notice or compare who's doing what because we're caught up in the beauty of their movement together.

In marriage, God calls husbands to lead and wives to submit to the grace of the dance. The rhythm is set as they live under the control of the Holy Spirit.

Now, some wives might be thinking, *What about when my husband doesn't lead well? He steps on my toes.* There will be times when you can't figure out his sense of direction as you move through life. But keep communicating, keep trying.

Just keep dancing.

Hers

What if he stumbles and falls? What if he misses the marks of real manhood? Show him the same mercy that God has shown you. Whisper in his ear what the rhythm of the song is, so he can hear it and lead according to the Holy Spirit.

Just keep dancing.

What if he has rejected the gospel or chooses to live contrary to God's Word? 1 Peter 3:1 to 2 says,

Likewise, wives, be subject to your own husbands, so that even if some do not obey the word, they may be won without a word by the conduct of their wives, when they see your respectful and pure conduct.

You don't need to preach at him. Instead, by your actions, show him the inner beauty of godliness. The presence of Christ *in* you being lived *through* you can draw his heart toward God.

Just keep dancing.

And what about your role as a wife? If you are feeling dissatisfied or defeated in your marriage, remember that a covenant says *I will*, not *I will if you do*. Seek wise, biblical counsel and take some lessons to get in step again.

Then you can keep dancing.

Maybe you're a wife who is enjoying a healthy marriage right now. Be thankful, and remain faithful to your God-given calling. Also, accept the responsibility that comes with maturity—to show younger women how to grow in God's grace and in the marks of real womanhood.

You keep dancing too, and teach them how it's done.

Scripture shows us that a woman's true beauty comes from within, in womanhood marked by the pursuit of holiness and the presence of

Christ-like character. And when a wife embraces the priority of the home and the practice of submission, her marriage flourishes in step with her husband. Together, they reflect the love of Christ for the church and the grace of the gospel in the home.

Holy Spirit,
Keep us in step with the song of redemption
as we grow in the timeless beauty
that only comes with the pursuit of holiness.
May we as women always remember that we are
daughters of God first and foremost.
Amen.

Four

REDEEMING INTIMACY

You've probably had the uncomfortable experience of a little too much eye contact with someone. Maybe you've just walked into a store or restaurant. As you glance around, you accidentally lock eyes with a person who happens to be looking at you at the very same moment. It takes you both by surprise, so you quickly turn away. And for seemingly no reason, you feel awkward.

That's because eye contact brings you face-to-face with a person. It's a form of intimacy. And without the context of a relationship, being face-to-face with someone can make you feel vulnerable. The unexpected intimacy of eye contact with a stranger is more than either of you bargained for. You may find yourself asking: *What are they thinking? Do I have something stuck in my teeth? Do they know me from somewhere?*

Now think back to when you met someone you wanted to get to know—a friend or perhaps your spouse. Maybe you had an awkward feeling at first, but you sensed a connection. You anticipated the chance to develop a relationship face-to-face, and so did they.

When intimacy is awkward, we feel it.
And when intimacy works, it's a beautiful thing.

As we continue to examine the meaning of the gospel in the home, we come face-to-face with our brokenness. We saw in chapter one how marriage isn't broken, people are. And when broken people get married, they're simply broken together. The problem isn't that marriage has a flawed *design*. It's that we haven't fulfilled the design in the way God alone *defines*. We desperately need the hope offered to us in the gospel, not only in our individual lives, but also in our marriages.

Here's the good news: The Creator who designed and defined marriage is also the Redeemer of the brokenness we bring with us into marriage.

• • •

Before we go on, let's be clear: in this chapter, *intimacy* is not a code word for *sex*. These are two different things, although they are related.

The sexual union of a man and a woman is something God designed to be enjoyed and stewarded within the covenant of marriage. But intimacy is so much more than just that. Intimacy is deeper and more meaningful than sex itself.

You can experience intimacy in relationships where sex would be inappropriate, outside of God's design. For example, as you keep reading, you may ask yourself: *How is my intimacy with God? With my parents, my brothers, my sisters? With my most trusted friends?* And of course, since this book is about marriage, we encourage you to ask: *How is my intimacy with my spouse?*

When we talk about intimacy, we might use other words like *together* or *companionship* or *being accepted* or *fully known*. These describe what relational intimacy really is.

It involves vulnerability.
It requires trust.
It means being open and transparent.

These characteristics of relational intimacy form the foundation for sexual intimacy. So we don't start with sex. We start with the covenant relationship that brings husband and wife face-to-face in the intimacy of marriage.

Back to the Love Story Before Brokenness

Back in chapter one, we explored the creation love story before brokenness. We're going to revisit that story in Genesis 1 to learn what the Scripture teaches us about intimacy. In the beginning, everything comes to life by the very breath of God, and we hear the rhythm of a poem with a repeated phrase:

"And God saw that it was good."

Light and darkness.
Heavens and earth.
Water and dry land.

"And God saw that it was good."

Plants and trees.
Seasons and stars.
Fish and birds and livestock.

"And God saw that it was good."

Then came Adam. And in Genesis 2:18, the rhythm of the poem is interrupted: "It is not good that the man should be alone."

Wait a minute. *Not good?*

It's not that Adam wasn't good, but rather that the opportunity for human intimacy was missing. God wasn't finished creating yet. The story wasn't finished unfolding yet.

So let's keep reading through verses 18 to 25:

> Then the Lord God said, "It is not good that the man should be alone; I will make him a helper fit for him."
>
> Now out of the ground the Lord God had formed every beast of the field and every bird of the heavens and brought them to the man to see what he would call them. And whatever the man called every living creature, that was its name. The man gave names to all livestock and to the birds of the heavens and to every beast of the field.
>
> But for Adam there was not found a helper fit for him. So the Lord God caused a deep sleep to fall upon the man, and while he slept took one of his ribs and closed up its place with flesh. And the rib that the Lord God had taken from the man he made into a woman and brought her to the man.
>
> Then the man said,
> > "This at last is bone of my bones
> > > and flesh of my flesh;
> > she shall be called Woman,
> > > because she was taken out of Man."
>
> Therefore a man shall leave his father and his mother and hold fast to his wife, and they shall become one flesh. And the man and his wife were both naked and were not ashamed.

No awkward eye contact here. Adam and Eve came face-to-face with each other in the beauty of intimacy God created and intended.

....

Todd: She has my number!

I first met my wife when she was about to graduate high school. During my sophomore year in college, I was speaking at a chapel service that she happened to attend. Following the chapel, I noticed this girl making eye contact with me. She then confidently approached me and said that she was extremely interested in attending the university that I was attending. She asked if she could call me and ask some questions about my school and without hesitation I gave her my number. Later, she confessed that she had never even heard of my university before that day, but she just needed an excuse to ask for my number. Needless to say, I might have been deceived but I was not disappointed! We spent the next few months talking over the phone with 162 miles between us. Our relationship was growing even though we were not even dating. Intimacy was being established as we talked about our childhood experiences, hopes and dreams, family, and our relationship with Jesus. After a few months of talking, we finally went on our first date! Man, I was completely taken by her. Not only was she beautiful, funny, loved Jesus, and had a desire to spend the rest of her life in ministry, but she was also easy to talk to. I knew within the first few conversations that I would spend the rest of my life with this woman. She asked for my number over 18 years ago . . . and she still has my number today!

....

God's design for intimacy reveals the beauty of oneness.

No doubt, Adam had noticed how all the creatures in the garden of Eden had suitable mates. He had surveyed them all. He had named them all. And in so doing, you get the sense that he longed for a companion to call his own.

Adam was alone, and it wasn't good.

But God wasn't finished creating yet. Fast forward through a deep sleep and a supernatural surgery, and Adam wakes up to . . . *Wow*. A helper fit for him.

Let's take time to focus on some important details here.

First, God forms and fashions Eve from one of Adam's ribs. Charles Spurgeon, a popular British preacher during the 1800s, noted:

Eve is not made out of his head as to top him, not out of his feet as to be trampled on by him, but out of his side to be equal with him, under his arm to be protected, and near his heart to be loved.[14]

What a beautiful description of companionship by God's design.

Second, the word *helper* is used most often in the Scriptures in reference to God himself—particularly the help of Holy Spirit in the life of the believer. It literally refers to one who provides what is lacking, or to something that is opposite. That's the word in Genesis to describe the relationship of Eve to Adam, of a wife to her husband: she's a helper fit for him.

Tim Keller explains this in his book, *The Meaning of Marriage*:

---

14. Citation of Spurgeon in G.J. Wenham, *Genesis 1-15* (Waco, TX: Word, 1987), 69.

They are like two pieces of a puzzle that fit together because they are not exactly alike nor randomly different, but they are differentiated such that together they can create a complete whole.[15]

It's unmistakable: God made this union, this understanding, this picture of marriage. God created the relationship between Adam and Eve to experience connection. Note that Adam didn't make his helper. Adam didn't identify and define his helper. God did. God is the designer of intimacy.

Third, in the details of Genesis 2:23, Adam is so overwhelmed that he exclaims, *at last*. The Hebrew words here communicate the idea of percussive rhythm.

Drum roll!
Cue love song.

It's like when you hear the first few beats of a great song, and you recognize it immediately. Then the guitar starts strumming, the bass fires up, the piano gets going, and you know it's going to be epic.

At a wedding, it's the moment just before the bride comes down the aisle. The bridesmaids have already made the processional to the front of the church. The groom is there—waiting, waiting, waiting—until finally, the room becomes hushed. Then that song you know so well starts playing. The congregation stands to their feet. Heads turn to the back door as it swings open. And here comes the bride.

At last! You're the one I've been waiting for.

Adam cannot contain his excitement when he encounters Eve face-to-face. He continues the poem of creation with lyrics for Eve:

---

15. Timothy and Kathy Keller, *The Meaning of Marriage*, (New York, NY: Penguin Books, 2013), 174.

bone of my bones and flesh of my flesh. He recognizes the intimacy God has created to satisfy his longing for a companion, a helper fit for him.

The Intimacy of Connecting Face-to-Face

Like Adam, we find joy and delight when we experience God's design for intimacy. When a couple stands face-to-face to make their vows with each other before the Lord, there is a divine union. There is a knitting together of two souls. There is a connection that is far more significant than legal status.

God has created them for a perfect fit—emotionally, spiritually, and physically. And in this relationship, God designed sex to fulfill the intimacy he designed. Sex consummates the marriage covenant that unites husband and wife as one flesh.

This is why sex outside of marriage is so damaging to the human heart—because it lacks the fullness of intimacy God intended. There's more going on than physical pleasure. In God's design, there's also an emotional and spiritual connection at the deepest level of who we are.

To experience God's design for marriage, we have to make intimacy a priority. We don't live independently of one another. We don't give the best of ourselves to other people or other things. We don't live like roommates. No, we are designed for oneness.

We can't mistake the intimacy of the wedding ceremony in Genesis 2:24, which says, "a man shall leave his father and his mother and hold fast to his wife." Remember when we looked at the old words from Shakespeare's day, *leave* and *cleave?* To cleave, or to hold fast, carries the idea of being glued together. You're permanently attached. It's like welding two pieces of metal; they become one.

It has been well said that "marriage mathematics is one plus one equals one." The husband and wife become one flesh. God designed marriage to experience this bond of intimacy.

• • •

All of us, married or not, can experience intimacy with God. Despite our brokenness, he offers salvation to redeem us and restore oneness in our relationship with him. This opportunity is afforded to each of us in Jesus Christ. We can grow in oneness with God, our Father, through his Son, our Savior, by the indwelling power of his Holy Spirit, our ultimate Helper.

We have previously looked at Genesis 1:27, which says that God created male and female in his own image. Did you ever stop to think what that image brings with it? *Oneness.*

In the design of intimacy, when image bearers of God are united together, there's a portrayal of God's own oneness. Now, this can be hard to get your head around. But the essence is that God exists as three persons in complete unity and intimacy: Father, Son, and Holy Spirit. This is what we mean when we talk about the Trinity. God is three in one.

We find the Hebrew word *echad,* meaning one, used to describe God in Deuteronomy 6:4. "Hear, O Israel: The LORD our God, the LORD is one."

Did you know that the same Hebrew word appears in Genesis 2:24? "They shall become *one* flesh." *Echad.* As men and women made in the image of God's oneness, we reflect oneness in the intimacy of marriage. It's part of the portrait of the gospel in the home—both for us to enjoy, and for us to bear witness to a fallen world who looks upon the mystery of marriage with great wonder. When people see oneness in a Christian marriage, they see the very glory of God revealed.

God's gift of intimacy reveals his unconditional love.

We read in the story of Adam and Eve that God designed intimacy as a solution to the need for companionship. In this design, we see God's gift; he provided what Adam could not. In Genesis 2:25, we begin to understand that this gift is unconditional and powerful, as it says, "the man and his wife were both naked and were not ashamed."

What is this verse talking about? Is it a physical thing? Absolutely. But it's more than that. The idea of being naked is to be vulnerable, to be transparent, to be fully revealed, to be fully known. This is a profound gift.

In our broken reality today, why are we so obsessed with clothes? Because clothes hide us. They cover up what we don't want others to see. But in the love story before brokenness, Adam and Eve had such intimacy that they didn't need clothes. They could stand face-to-face and be completely vulnerable, completely transparent. Their bodies and souls were bare before each other, with no shame, no guilt.

Do you realize that God knows you this intimately? He knows *you*.

He doesn't just know the well dressed, put-together you that the rest of us greet with high-fives and hugs.

He doesn't just know the I-need-coffee you that your family sees when you wake up the in the morning.

He doesn't just know the stressed-out you that stomps in the door after the wheels come off your big project at work.

God knows the deepest recesses of *you*.
The *you* that you hide.
The *you* that you're afraid to show anyone.
The *you* that feels naked and ashamed.

God knows all of you, and yet he loves you unconditionally—the evidence of that love being that he sent his Son to die for you.

This is the greatest gift of intimacy: to be fully known and completely loved. In marriage and family relationships, this gift brings an unbelievable blessing.

Connor: Personal Story

Initially, Mary and I both thought that intimacy and our marriage would be primarily about candlelight dinners, long walks on the beach and late night conversations together. Those things are great, and we have experienced our share of them. In our marriage however, our intimacy has been built far more often from difficult conversations, confession of sin and the safety of grace and forgiveness that we have each experienced one from the other. That's where God has given us the deepest sense of true, lasting intimacy. That is "naked and unashamed." There's something powerful for me that my wife Mary knows me and she loves me. She doesn't know just the funny and kind and outgoing Connor. No, she knows all of the other darker versions as well. She knows me and she loves me. This is a gift of intimacy and a blessing that is received when we walk in it. This is powerful. Fully known, completely loved. Intimacy.

In our brokenness, it's a beautiful thing to be able to say, *I am fully known and yet completely loved.* In marriage as God designed it, the gift of intimacy means that a husband and wife can be naked and unashamed, emotionally and spiritually.

But here's the thing: This kind of vulnerability requires that we embrace marriage as a covenant. We have already looked at the difference between a contract and a covenant.

A contract has stipulations. A contract says, *I expect this, and if you don't fulfill that, then I'm not going to do what you expect of me.* It's a transaction. This for that.

But a covenant says, *I am going to fulfill my promise to you no matter what.*

In the first chapter of this book, we described the difference this way:

A covenant is binding, but a contract is conditional.
A covenant is based on giving, but a contract is based on receiving.
A covenant is about serving, but a contract is about being served.
A covenant says, *I will,* but a contract says, *I will if you do.*

In order to experience God's gift of intimacy in marriage, a covenant says to your spouse, *I know you, and I love you just the same. And I'm here to stay.* It's a gift with no strings attached.

Maybe you've stood up in a room of friends and family, face-to-face with your beloved, and you have said vows before God that sounded something like this:

I take you to be my wedded husband;
I take you to be my wedded wife;
To have and to hold,
From this day forward,
For better, for worse,
For richer, for poorer,
In sickness and in health;
To love and to cherish
As long as we both shall live.

Did you notice any *ifs, ands* or *buts* in those words? No—because those are the words of a covenant. When we live as husband and wife in this covenant called marriage, it provides a safe place to be fully known and completely loved. And intimacy flourishes.

When you read the creation story, it doesn't say anywhere that Adam and Eve were worthy of God creating them, sustaining them, and giving them companionship with each other. They didn't earn that. They didn't deserve that. God initiated and provided their opportunity to enjoy each other face-to-face.

Husbands and wives, let this sink in: God's love for you is not contingent upon anything you do; it's covenant love—no prenuptial agreement, no conditions, no strings attached. When you practice that kind of love toward your spouse, it fuels your marriage. That's intimacy in action.

Connor: Pursuing Intimacy . . .

As a pastor, I do a lot of marriage counseling. So many couples come in, and one of the things we talk about is physical intimacy—because their sex life is not good. While sex isn't the be-all and end-all of marriage, it's often a great indicator of the health of a relationship.

So we'll start talking, and I'll ask, *How's this going for you?*

And do you know what kind of answers I hear? *Well, our 9-year-old sleeps in bed with us.* Or, *We're too tired after we watch TV.* Seriously?

These couples are setting themselves up for failure. Intimacy doesn't magically happen. Create the mood for romance early in your day. Flirt with your spouse. Have an actual conversation—more than *Uh-huh, yeah, uh-huh . . . Wait, what was that?*

Also develop a schedule that works for your family, then follow it. Tuck your kids into their *own* beds at a reasonable hour.

Dream out loud with each other. Confess your faults. Give thanks for the little things that bring joy to your lives. Pray with and pray for one another. This is friendship. This is real intimacy.

For the record, I'll just say that sex in marriage is not like the movies. So keep it real. And remember that your sex life can never exceed the level of intimacy you cultivate with your spouse.

....

The Risk of Working Shoulder-to-Shoulder

Without question, marriage takes work. A covenant requires commitment. It's not as easy as a walk down the aisle. What happens often is that we go through phases in our marriage. We start out face-to-face, heart-to-heart. We're on honeymoon for a while. Then intimacy fades when life gets busy and stress invades.

Kids enter the picture.
Careers enter the picture.
Bills enter the picture.
Health issues enter in the picture.

We're in this together, we tell ourselves. And we mean well—showing a unified front and all. But our marriage has become about managing life, not so much face-to-face as shoulder-to-shoulder. The covenant of marriage begins to give way to the expectations of a contract.

Maybe it sounds like this: *We're hanging in there for the kids. We're sticking together for the sake of the family. We're going to do this as long as we can. When we get the kids graduated, then we'll see if we can make it. Hopefully we'll have time to enjoy each other.*

When this happens, you've traded intimacy for survival.

But God has given us as husbands and wives something with far greater potential than household management and getting the kids through school. He has created the opportunity for friendship and companionship—to share life together *while* we do those things.

The book, *The Seven Principles for Making Marriage Work*, revealed staggering results from a survey of men and women. Sociologist John Gottman, known for his study of married couples, identified the determining factor in whether wives feel satisfied with the sex, romance, and passion in their marriage. Can you guess what it is? *Friendship*. By a factor of 70 percent.[16]

What's even more fascinating is that husbands responded to the survey in the same way, by the same percentage. So it turns out that men and women are from the same planet after all.

Friendship matters.
And the stronger the friendship, the deeper the intimacy.

Over time, if we neglect the marriage relationship God has entrusted to us, we make a terrible trade without even realizing it. We give up face-to-face intimacy for shoulder-to-shoulder work. And before we know it, there's a gap—a separation—that starts to occur. We're still alongside each other, but not as close as we used to be. Before we know it:

Kids come between us.
Careers come between us.
Bills come between us.
Health issues come between us.

And then, when conflict arises, we turn back-to-back.

---

16. John M. Gottman and Nan Silver, *The Seven Principles for Making Marriage Work* (New York: Three Rivers Press, 1999), 17.

The Pain of Turning Back-to-Back

Too many marriages reach the painful place where husbands and wives have stopped investing in each other. Not only have they lost the connection of face-to-face intimacy—they're not even shoulder-to-shoulder, heading in the same direction anymore. Now they're turned away from each other, pulling apart. There's no covenant love between them, and even the contract is stretched thin.

She has one idea about what to do, and he has a completely different one. She has one desire for their family, and he has another. Anger turns to frustration and then turns to bitterness. Even if they're living under the same roof, they're not truly living together.

If this describes your marriage, let today be the day you turn shoulder-to-shoulder again, facing the same direction. God desires to redeem and restore the intimacy he created for you to experience in your marriage. You may need help from a pastor or counselor to reorient your relationship. And then, actively look for moments when you can begin to connect face-to-face again. Fight for those moments. Go on date nights. Pursue each other emotionally. Show kindness. Extend forgiveness. Be vulnerable. Chase after the heart of your spouse.

• • •

The reason we drift from face-to-face connection is because, at the end of the day, we are broken people. Sin interrupted intimacy in the garden of Eden. God said not to eat the forbidden fruit, but Adam and Eve ate it anyway.

That choice came with consequences in their relationship as husband and wife, and in their relationship with God. Adam and Eve felt shame for the first time. Instead of experiencing intimacy with each other and with God, they felt naked and exposed. So they needed a cover-up. Fig leaves were the best they could find.

With the sin of Adam and Eve, humanity turned its back on the

Creator. At this point in the story, we begin to see the self-absorption of humanity. We mask our true selves. We fear being known because of the guilt of our sin. We hide from God.

But the original gift of intimacy we saw in the garden becomes possible again when we allow Christ to redeem our brokenness.

God's redemption of intimacy reveals the grace of the gospel.

In marriage, after we have turned shoulder-to-shoulder, or even back-to-back, how can we restore face-to-face intimacy? The answer comes when you saturate yourself with the gospel of Jesus. When you rest in the grace of Christ. When you understand and admit that sin separates you from God, there is a spiritual gap.

You can't cover it with fig leaves.
You can't hide it and hope God won't notice.
You're broken, and you don't have what it takes to fix yourself.

But just like when Adam was alone in the garden, God isn't finished creating yet. The story isn't finished unfolding yet. We know this because Romans 5:8 says: ". . . but God shows his love for us in that while we were still sinners, Christ died for us." In other words, Jesus Christ entered our back-to-back relationship with God while we were sinners, separated from him.

God's covenant love is not based on anything we do. He set about solving the problem of brokenness, making a way to restore the intimacy that was interrupted in Eden. He did not wait for us to get covered up or cleaned up.

Do you know what that means for you? That God embraces you in your nakedness, in your shame, and in the guilt of your sin. He says, *I know you fully, and I love you completely. I see the worst of you, yet I'm still going to give you the best of me.*

You don't have to be ashamed. You don't have to carry guilt. You don't have to hide from love like this.

We come to a better understanding of face-to-face intimacy when we recognize how God's love takes initiative and action to redeem us. It enters our mess. Do you remember where you were when Jesus rescued you? A mess. You say, *I hadn't done that much wrong.* But you were a mess. You know the weakness and wickedness of your own heart. And yet Jesus Christ entered into your mess. He initiated love and saved you.

This is redemption—that God came seeking Adam and Eve in the garden after they had sinned. He moved toward them. He closed the gap in their relationship. And in Christ, he moves toward you. He wants to close the gap in your relationship with him.

When you accept redemption in Christ, you experience the amazing grace of the gospel, fully known and completely loved by God. That's vertical reconciliation from heaven to earth, from God to you.

For every one of us, married or not, this is where intimacy begins. We embrace this covenant love of God to experience vertical intimacy.

Now, you might wonder, *What does that have to do with marriage?* Here's how it plays out. When you rest in vertical reconciliation of intimacy between you and God, you are free to look horizontally across the gap between you and your spouse. You can come face-to-face with your husband or your wife. You can show the real you. Vulnerable. Transparent. Because you are accepted and embraced by God, you don't have to fear being rejected by another human being.

You might think, *What if my spouse doesn't embrace me like God embraces me?* Remember that you are held in the covenant embrace of God. You didn't deserve it. You didn't earn it. So extend God's grace by showing unconditional, covenant love toward your spouse—not based on whether they embrace you in return.

Redeeming Intimacy

Redeemed intimacy is a real possibility. Not only that, it reveals the grace of the gospel in the home.

• • •

As you're reading this chapter, you may be in conflict with God. You may be living back-to-back, looking the other direction from the unconditional love he has extended to you. Would you have the courage today to turn and look to him? This is the invitation of the gospel.

God desires intimacy with you . . .

Face-to-face.

Perhaps in your marriage, you're holding on to expectations: *I will if you do.* You've living under a contract rather than a covenant, which means that you and your spouse are not free to be vulnerable and transparent with each other.

Love unconditionally as you have been loved by God . . .

Face-to-face.

Or maybe you're on the brink of calling it quits and getting a divorce. You are not beyond hope. You are not beyond forgiveness or healing in Christ. Make the choice, however hard, however humbling, to turn toward each other.

God has made a way to redeem your brokenness and restore your intimacy . . .

Face-to-face.

If you have already gone through the pain of divorce, you may think you'll never let yourself be vulnerable again. Stop hiding in fear and rest in the grace of Christ. Pray for God's healing of your heart.

Seek the Holy Spirit as your helper and companion . . .

Face-to-face.

Maybe your marriage is shoulder-to-shoulder. You are trying to keep things together but you're actually drifting apart from your husband or wife, just trying to keep up with life.

Take time together to examine your priorities . . .

Face-to-face.

Perhaps you have accepted that you are fully known and completely loved by God. And your marriage is growing in the gift of intimacy that comes with unconditional love. Don't take it for granted.

Cherish and cultivate God's gift of intimacy . . .

Face-to-face.

Wherever you find yourself today, let the gospel saturate your soul with the assurance that you are fully known and completely loved.

God's design for intimacy reveals the beauty of oneness in the mystery of marriage. His gift of intimacy comes with no strings attached—the unconditional example of covenant love between a husband and wife. And, his redemption of intimacy reveals the grace of the gospel in our individual lives and in the home.

Redeemer God,
Thank you for lavishing your love on us,
despite our brokenness.
You took initiative and action
to restore our relationship with you,
that we might experience the grace of the gospel
and the gift of intimacy in marriage.
May we be faithful to such love.
Amen.

Five

BE FRUITFUL AND MULTIPLY

Click. Whether it's on your Facebook feed or a website, you've probably fallen for a few click-bait headlines about having kids. You know the kind we're talking about—the top 10 surprises or 18 reasons or 37 quotes that make you smile and cringe at the same time. Basically, it's a run-down of the best and worst and scariest moments of being a parent.

Usually it begins with a crazy title like this:

Parenthood Reality Check: Incredible Things Nobody Ever Told You About How Your Little Darling Changes Everything

You will . . .

- Experience a love more powerful than you ever imagined.
- Do more on less sleep than seems humanly possible.
- Search for a lost pacifier like it's a million-dollar lottery ticket.

- Laugh more than you ever have in your life.
- Talk about poop as if it's a perfectly normal topic of conversation.
- Find out just how short your temper can be.
- Gain a whole new respect for your parents.
- End up with a Netflix account that suggests only kids' shows.
- And some days, look at your spouse and wonder: What on earth were we thinking?!

All that sounds about right based on our experience. There's no question that parenthood changes you.

But this list misses the most important reason the Bible states for having children. We find it in Psalm 127:3 to 5.

> **Behold, children are a heritage from the Lord,**
> **the fruit of the womb a reward.**
> **Like arrows in the hand of a warrior**
> **are the children of one's youth.**
> **Blessed is the man**
> **who fills his quiver with them!**
> **He shall not be put to shame**
> **when he speaks with his enemies in the gate.**

Children truly are a gift from the Lord. The word *heritage* in the Hebrew language could also be translated as gift. And, as the saying goes, they're a gift that keeps on giving. Proverbs 17:6 talks about the generational nature of family when it says, "Grandchildren are the crown of the aged, and the glory of children is their fathers."

So, whatever the cultural reasons for having children, Scripture teaches us God's greater purpose for blessing our lives with children.

Now, before we move into this chapter, we want to recognize that talking about children can be painful for couples facing infertility. And it can be hard for anyone who has ever lost a child. If this is your experience, then may God's comfort abound for you.

You may prefer to come back and read this chapter at a later time. When you're ready, we hope you'll find insight here to strengthen your family relationships—including those with your parents, your extended family, and loved ones you have officially or unofficially adopted as your own.

Whatever your circumstances, hold on to the important idea here: Children are a gift from the Lord—and that means *you* are his gift too. No matter your age, the fact that you were born into this world is part of a God-given heritage, and part of how he reveals the grace of the gospel in the home.

Todd: What Are We Supposed to Do Now?

When you have your first child, there are a lot of things they don't tell you. Emotionally, for example. The first time I held our newborn daughter, I knew immediately in that moment: *I am capable of murder. I could kill someone if they hurt this little girl.* Because I experienced a depth of love I just can't explain.

Then there was a moment of panic. *What in the world am I supposed to do now?* As my wife Adrian and I left the hospital, I remember thinking: *They're actually going to let us take her home! But we have no clue what we're doing.*

So we got safely settled in the car, and I drove maybe 18 miles an hour. Meanwhile, everyone else on the highway was driving like a maniac. Adrian sat in the backseat with our daughter as if that provided more protection.

We got home. We disinfected the entire place. Y'all know what I'm talking about. First-child stuff. And it seemed like every day we would ask ourselves: *What in the world are we supposed to do now?*

Well, let me say that 10 years and three kids later, we're still asking the same question. As our kids grow through different phases of life—and as my wife and I go through different seasons—there's always something we're walking into for the first time. So we're always asking: *What in the world are we supposed to do now? What is it that God has called us to do?*

....

When you hold a baby—or even when you hesitate to hold one because they seem so fragile—you immediately get a sense that life is a gift. Nobody has to explain that to you. You just get it.

Back in Genesis 1:26 to 27, we discover what's so unique about the gift of human life that sets us apart from all the rest of creation.

Then God said, "Let us make man in our image, after our likeness. And let them have dominion over the fish of the sea and over the birds of the heavens and over the livestock and over all the earth and over every creeping thing that creeps on the earth."

So God created man in his own image, in the image of God he created him; male and female he created them.

As we have been emphasizing throughout this book, every human being is created in the image of God. Male and female, we display the character, nature, and glory of God like nothing else.

Pause to think how massively important this is.

Consider the vastness of our universe.
Consider the wonders of the world, seen and unseen.

Be Fruitful and Multiply

Consider the amazing things discovered every day.
Consider the places that take your breath away.
And now consider the fact that none of these—not even one—
   bears the image of God. But you do.

Your life is a gift that reflects the image of God.

That's mind blowing, isn't it? It's overwhelming to recognize that your purpose is to display the image and glory of God.

And if that's the purpose of every human being, then what do you suppose is the ultimate purpose of the family? You guessed it: to display the image and glory of God—together. This basic understanding is crucial to helping you capture and experience God's vision for your family.

God's vision for the family
is to show his glory, not ours.

Not only did God create us to reflect his image and glory, he made us so that we would multiply his image and glory. When we look at Genesis 1:28, we begin to see God's vision for the family.

> And God blessed them. And God said to them, "Be fruitful and multiply and fill the earth and subdue it, and have dominion over the fish of the sea and over the birds of the heavens and over every living thing that moves on the earth."

Why does God say to be fruitful and multiply? Because he desires that his glory be revealed in his image bearers to fill all of creation, to fill the earth. God wants his glory shown everywhere. This is the essence of God's vision for the family.

Vision refers to a desired end or aim. What does the end look like? What is the aim or the trajectory? What are we shooting for? What's our vision?

Parents, we have to ask ourselves: *Is our vision the same as God's vision for our family?* We know what God's vision is—to display his glory. That means our families are not about us. Period. They are not about our glory, our desires, or our self-gratification.

When you look at your family, the structure of your home, the way you manage your calendar and order your life—what are you aiming for as a family?

When it comes to vision, we can be nearsighted. It's too easy to think only about today—whatever is immediate. And when it comes to parenting our kids, often we're only thinking about social acceptance. We're focused on our kids' behavior right now.

We want them to get the grade.
We want them to make good friends.
We want them to accomplish this specific task.
We want them to make the team.

But these are nearsighted things. If we're not careful, we'll spend the majority of our lives focused on a limited vision for our family.

Now, maybe some of us take a longer view. We think about accomplishments. We want our kids to get the good grades so they can get into college and prepare for a solid career. We want them to choose friends who will be a good influence in their lives. We want them to learn the importance of hard work, so they'll appreciate it when they make the team.

None of these things is wrong. But even if our family aims for the long view, we still come up short of the vision God desires for us. We've got to look beyond the long view to the eternal view—that our lives, our children, and our families are gifts *from* God and are *for* his glory.

Do you realize that your children were created for eternity? You've been given a very short time with them. As a parent, how many times have you thought, *Wow, they're growing up so fast*. Blink, and they'll be gone. They are gifts on loan to you.

So, with the short window of time you're given with your family, what can you accomplish for eternity? How will you shape the hearts of your children during the time you have with them?

Connor: Enjoying the Catch

My family loves to go fishing, especially bass fishing. When I take my kids fishing, I'll cast out and set the hook, then hand off the rod and reel to my son or daughter. They get to enjoy reeling in and catching the fish.

Now, we all know who did the work to catch the fish. I'm the one who decided where we were going to fish. I'm the one who drove there. I'm the one who purchased the rods, reels, and tackle. I'm the one who baited the hook. I'm the one who made the cast. Ultimately, I'm even the one who set the hook on the fish. My kids are simply enjoying the fruit of my work.

One day, I realized this is a great picture of God's vision for my family. God has done all the work. He is sovereign. He made everything possible, and yet here I am, enjoying the catch.

Why do we set our sights short of God's vision for our families? Once again, we find the answer in the garden of Eden. Through Adam and Eve, sin entered the world. We have already seen how sin brought tragic consequences for their relationship with each other and with God.

As the story of Genesis unfolds, we read in chapter 4 how Adam and Eve became parents. If Facebook had been around then, we would have seen photos of their son, Cain, who loved to play in the dirt. And we would have cooed when little brother Abel came along; he absolutely adored animals.

Like cute kids everywhere, Cain and Abel were born to reflect the image of God. But they were also born with a sinful nature that seeks to fulfill selfish desires. The same is true for all of us. Within us, a constant battle rages between God's glory and our own.

This battle played out in the deadly story of Cain and Abel. One day, in a fit of jealous pride that led to rage, Cain murdered his brother.

Murder is the opposite of fruitful.

Death is subtraction, not multiplication.

God's vision for the family was broken in an instant.

Today, you may find yourself thinking: *Yeah, my family is a bit of a wreck.* Maybe this describes the family you grew up in. Or maybe this describes you and your children. Or both.

If you've never thought about a vision for your family, there's good news. The same gospel that promises to redeem our brokenness as men and women can also restore our vision to become the kind of family that shows the world God's glory.

In his grace, God shows us what a transformed family life looks like when we live it out. So, as we continue this chapter, we will explore some practical ways to reconcile family relationships. God's Word not only teaches us as parents how to relate to our children; it also teaches us as children—even adult children—how to relate to our parents.

In God's vision for the family, parents hold a place of honor for a lifetime.

We began this chapter with a reminder that children are a gift from the Lord, which means *you* are his gift too. You may not be a kid anymore, but the fact remains that you wouldn't be here if you didn't have parents.

Be Fruitful and Multiply

It's important to keep this in mind as we look at what the apostle Paul wrote to a young and influential church in the ancient city of Ephesus. We have already examined Paul's words to husbands and wives from Ephesians chapter 5. Now we turn to Ephesians 6:1 to 4 for instruction in family life.

Children, obey your parents in the Lord, for this is right. "Honor your father and mother" (this is the first commandment with a promise), "that it may go well with you and that you may live long in the land." Fathers, do not provoke your children to anger, but bring them up in the discipline and instruction of the Lord.

We're going to work our way through what these verses mean, but the big idea here is about the relationship between parents and children. What we will learn together is not simply about you as a parent and the way you relate to your children. It also has to do with how you honor your parents—because this is part of God's vision for the family.

In this spirit, Paul begins with: *children, obey your parents*. When children hear this command, you know exactly what happens. They look for an escape clause. No doubt you did. Obey is not a popular word except on Shepard Fairey t-shirts—and even then, it's used in irony.

But notice the next part of that phrase: *in the Lord.*

Then think about this relative to your childhood, and also now as you raise your children: Obedience, or the lack of it, has more to do with your relationship to Jesus than it does your relationship to your parents. Sure, you raised your hands in worship. You went to church camp. You read your Bible daily. But what about obeying your parents?

Childhood obedience demonstrates trust in God who has given parents authority and responsibility in family life. Young people cannot claim to be walking with Jesus while being disobedient and disrespectful to their parents. It's a contradiction. This is why the verse says, "Children, obey your parents *in the Lord*, for this is right."

Parents, the number-one indicator of whether our kids are walking with Jesus is how they relate to us. This is huge.

Maybe you're wondering: What is Christ doing in the heart of my kids? How can I tell if Jesus is doing something in their lives? You'll see it, first of all, in how they relate to you. And if you don't see it—well, we'll be talking more about that a bit later in this chapter.

With that said, it's important to know what obedience is *not*.

First, it's not when a parent or guardian leads a child to a place of sin, and certainly not into immoral or illegal behavior. A child is not required to obey in those moments—not based on opinion or disagreement with a parent, but based on clear distinctions of right and wrong.

As parents, we will be wrong sometimes. Our children may obey us out of respect, in the Lord. But when we recognize that we've been wrong, we can model the importance of admitting our mistakes and asking for forgiveness. This allows our children to see God's grace at work in us.

Second, obedience means not having to be asked seven, eight, nine, or ten times. If we don't see a first-time response, then we're not seeing obedience—we're seeing a child forced to comply or threatened by escalating consequences.

Parents, if we see this kind of resistance in our children, we have to take a look at ourselves. Are we modeling obedience to authority? Or do we sometimes say things that undercut figures of authority—perhaps regarding work, or church, or the government? Do we automatically side with our children when there's a problem at school, or do we consider how they might have contributed to the problem?

The training ground for a child to become a responsible adult—an adult who contributes to society—is at home. If we don't teach them what it means to obey authority, they are going to have a hard time when they get older.

Speaking of getting older, let's look closely at the next part of the passage from Ephesians 6:

> "Honor your father and mother" (this is the first commandment with a promise), "that it may go well with you and that you may live long in the land."

In this verse, Paul quotes one of the Ten Commandments recorded in Deuteronomy 5:16. This is the first commandment with a promise attached to it—a blessing. And notice that it doesn't say to love, to be fond of, or even to agree with. It says to *honor*.

This word *honor* literally means to give the proper weight to something. We give our parents the proper respect because of the position they hold in our lives. Not necessarily because they were good parents—because maybe they weren't.

You may be dealing with the wounds of being poorly parented, and you're wondering, *how do I honor someone I don't respect?* And chances are, even if you had good parents, they weren't perfect—and your relationship isn't perfect because we're all broken people. But that's not the point here.

We are to honor our mothers and fathers because of the position God has given them. We extend grace to them. We show them the same love and mercy we have received in Jesus Christ. This honor continues for a lifetime; we don't outgrow it.

So, what does honor look like in practical terms? Let's explore four ways children can honor their moms and dads. These are principles to teach your children and model for them.

1. **Obey and respect.** In childhood, walk in obedience and respect. This means not rolling your eyes, sighing, and

acting out of obligation. This means saying, through your actions, *I respect the position God has given you in my life.*

2. **Involve and invite.** In young adulthood, seek wise counsel in making life decisions. Rather than parents hearing big news through the grapevine, share the inside scoop with them. They know you well and still want what's best for you.

3. **Care and provide.** As we get older, our role and responsibility shifts within the family. As a child, we were the ones being provided and cared for. But eventually, our parents may need us to become their providers and caregivers.

4. **Remember and tell.** Let's remember the legacy of our parents' lives, and pass it on to our children and grandchildren. Celebrate the family heritage. Keep it alive through special traditions and stories that instill memories and character for generations to come.

When obedience and honor are valued, God's vision for the family is realized in flourishing relationships between children and their parents. God intends flourishing relationships to last a lifetime and be passed on for generations. They are spiritually fruitful, and they multiply.

But that's not all we learn from Ephesians 6. As we read further, we discover how immediate family relationships can influence a child's most important relationship—with Jesus.

In God's vision for the family, parents nurture and train children to know Jesus.

Let's zoom in on Ephesians 6:4, which says: "Fathers, do not provoke your children to anger, but bring them up in the discipline and instruction of the Lord."

Be Fruitful and Multiply

This verse is not talking exclusively to fathers—because if you go back to the first verse, it says, children, obey your *parents*. Moms, you're not off the hook here, but dads, you set the example. You take the lead to raise your children up in the Lord. Don't check out and leave it to mom. You're both in this together.

We see two specific principles for parents here.

Christ-like Leadership

This principle begins with a warning: do not provoke your children to anger. This phrase literally could be translated, *stop an action in progress*. When you catch yourself inciting your anger in the heart of your child—stop! Otherwise, you'll only make them bitter at your position of authority in their life.

Remember a few chapters back when we said authority is like a bar of soap? The more you use it, the less you have left.

Now, this doesn't mean it's wrong to make your kids mad. When you discipline them, they're not necessarily going to be happy about it. They'll get mad. But don't provoke them. Don't incite a rebellious spirit that causes them to move in the opposite direction.

Every parent has crossed this line at one time or another. So how can you do better? Here are some ideas.

1. Correct your children in love rather than punishing them in anger. You've told them a dozen times: *Stop that*—bickering, punching, biting, teasing, you name it. *Do this*—be quiet, leave him alone, say you're sorry, be kind.

Yet the chaos continues. You lose your mind and your temper. *Why don't they just obey?* So you lash out in anger to punish their behavior. What they really need is correction that is motivated by love. Except you're not in the mood for it.

Sometimes, mom and dad, you need a time-out. You need to say: We're all going to our rooms, because I'm going to hurt you if we continue this conversation. And you take time to pray and think through your response. Talk to your spouse. Then when you've calmed down, you can address the issue in a loving way.

2. Let your children pursue their own dreams. If you're an ambitious parent, you might have all kinds of dreams for your children. Sports, school, friends, career—you've mapped out their entire lives, and you're steering them toward the future you imagine.

But kids need the opportunity to develop dreams of their own. God has given them unique personalities and gifts. If you don't let them flourish, you'll provoke your kids to rebellion. You'll ultimately push them away from you.

Your responsibility isn't to make certain dreams come true—yours or theirs. It's to be their biggest cheerleader. Instill character and help them discover God's plan for their lives.

3. Give your children the freedom to fail. Have you ever heard the saying, *failure is not an option?* Or maybe, *second place means first-place loser.* These are the opposite of what kids need to hear. If home is a no-fail zone, they feel constant pressure to perform.

But failure is one of the greatest teachers in life. If you don't give your children room to stumble and fall, you're going to crush them under the weight of unrealistic expectations. Nobody is perfect, not even you. So don't expect your kids to be either.

Dads, your sons and daughters long for your approval. They need to know that you love them no matter what, and that you're proud of them. Say *I love you*—for no other reason than that God gave them to you.

4. Remember that quality time is found in quantity time. One of the greatest myths of parenting is this: *We don't spend a lot of time, but it's quality.* Wrong. Because quality time is not something you initiate or plan. It's that one moment in a stretch of hours when a particular conversation happens—and you're there for it.

Be Fruitful and Multiply

Maybe you're out with your son or daughter walking through the woods, and you're just spending time together. You're talking, and all of a sudden, a question comes out of nowhere. A door is opened. But if you're not spending time together as a family, you're going to miss that moment when it happens. So make family time a priority

5. Practice what you preach. Kids can tell when you're faking it. They notice when you say one thing and do another, and hypocrisy will ultimately provoke them to anger.

Instead, let them see how you are learning to follow Jesus. As Galatians 5:22 to 23, says, "But the fruit of the Spirit is love, joy, peace, patience, kindness, goodness, faithfulness, gentleness, and self-control. Against such things there is no law." When you're living under the influence of the Holy Spirit, you're not going to provoke your kids to anger. Rather, your example will point them to Jesus.

Intentional Discipleship

When it comes to parenting our children, the second principle from Ephesians 6:4 says that we are to bring them up in the discipline and instruction of the Lord. *Bring them up* means to nurture them, to give them what they need to sustain them in life.

Picture it this way: You're in the woods, watching a mother bird interact with her chicks. She forms a nest. She finds food for her chicks. She protects them under her wing until they have grown big enough to leave the nest.

This is how the image of God is formed in the hearts of your children, as you nurture them in the love of Christ. It's intentional—which means that the structure of your life has to look different from families who are not seeking to raise their children in the Lord. When you're focused on education, sports, and social acceptance—when you're devoting your time to work more hours so you can give your kids the best of everything—you're at risk of making a spiritual trade-off.

It doesn't matter what opportunities your kids have or how much they accomplish. God's vision for your family is that your children would grow up to walk with Jesus. Nothing else can come close to that.

So, how can a parent aim for this? We find two words: discipline and instruction.

1. Discipline trains children toward God's best for them. Intentional discipleship happens through discipline. And the word *discipline* here could be translated *training*. Sometimes, when we think of discipline, we equate it with spankings and time-outs. But that's confusing discipline with punishment.

The gospel says that Jesus Christ, on the cross, took the punishment for sin. As parents, we have to understand that we're not responsible to punish our children for their bad behavior.

Instead, the word discipline implies *training*. We want our children to understand the way Jesus calls them to live. When they go out of bounds, there will be consequences—sometimes even painful ones. But rather than punishing their bad behavior, our responsibility is to remind them that sin is costly and robs us of joy. We're training them. We're navigating them toward God's best for them.

Todd: Daddy, Do You Love Me?

I'll never forget one particular time when my daughter asked: "Daddy, do you love me?"

"Yes, I love you with all my heart," I answered. But she's a thinker, always looking for the reason behind something, so I should have guessed she had more on her mind.

"But do you really love me?"

"Of course. I love you more than life itself."

"Would you ever want pain or harm to come to me?"

"Absolutely not. I would never want pain or harm to come to you."

I probably should have seen the next question coming. Because then she said: "Why in the world do you spank me and give me time-outs? It really hurts me when you do that."

Clever little girl.

Thankfully, the Holy Spirit got to me before I answered.

"I do those things because I am willing for you to experience temporary pain in the moment, if it means sparing you long-term pain in the future."

I wanted her to understand the difference between discipline and punishment. My desire was to train her toward the things of God.

....

2. Instruction emphasizes relational connections to encourage spiritual growth. Intentional discipleship happens in relationships. As parents, God entrusts us with the role of nurturing the spiritual lives of our children. We get to know their hearts. We encourage them to walk with Jesus. The goal is not for your kids to know *about* Jesus; the goal is for them to know Jesus.

Discipline needs to go hand in hand with instruction. If we're all about discipline and no instruction, we're going to give our kids a warped view of the gospel. They're going to think the gospel is about performance—that they have to earn God's approval and favor. In contrast, if we provide instruction to our kids without discipline, they're going to think the gospel is cheap; without consequences for sin, grace becomes meaningless.

Intentional discipleship marries discipline and instruction. Where discipline says, *that's not acceptable,* instruction says, *here's what God has for you.* Sometimes *no* is the best *yes.*

And think about this: When children are learning, they don't know how well they're doing unless somebody measures and gives feedback. So help them in this way. Sometimes, they'll need admonishment. Other times, when they do something well, praise them.

Ultimately, as moms and dads, we are entrusted with the nurturing and training our children to love and live for Jesus Christ. As C.S. Lewis wrote in *Mere Christianity*, "Every Christian is to become a little Christ."[17] And there is no better context for developing a "little Christ" than in the home. Through Christ-like leadership and intentional discipleship, we help form our sons and daughters to reflect the image and glory of God.

• • •

Parents, in God's vision for the family, there's no substitute for you. Your children are a gift from the Lord, entrusted to you.

Sadly, we live in culture of farmed-out families. Don't let yours be one of them. Accept the honor and responsibility of God's vision for your family.

> Church is good, but ministry leaders are not parents.
> Camp is good, but counselors are not parents.
> Sports teams are good, but coaches are not parents.
> Friends are good, but friends are not the same as parents.
> Social media, technology, gaming systems—they're fun, but they're awful parents.

Oh, your intentions may be good when you provide all these things for your children. You want to give them every opportunity. But if you're honest, sometimes you lean too much on these things because you're giving in, or you're giving up.

---

17. C. S. Lewis, *Mere Christianity* (London: Macmillan Publishing, 1978), 153.

Be Fruitful and Multiply

Parenting takes commitment. It takes an eternal view.
Focus your family on God's vision.

If your children have the most incredible church and camp experiences, and spiritually speaking, you think that covers it—don't be fooled. Moms and dads, you can't outsource your spiritual influence.
Focus your family on God's vision.

If your children have countless friends and a full calendar of sports and extracurricular activities, that's great. But don't allow those things to overshadow your priority to bring them up in the Lord.
Focus your family on God's vision.

If your family has the most incredible vacations and all the toys money can buy, but your children don't know Jesus, then they're at risk of a spiritual trade-off. Don't let that happen.
Focus your family on God's vision.

If your job causes you to spend so much time away from your family—stop. Your relationship with your children is now or never. It won't wait. You may need to change perspectives, change jobs, or even change your address to a smaller house.
Focus your family on God's vision.

And finally, if your family is mess—either the one you grew up in, or the one you're trying desperately to hold together—then by God's grace, let today be a new beginning. Choose obedience and honor over chaos and disrespect.
Focus your family on God's vision.

We are broken people. Sometimes we mask our brokenness by projecting the image of a family that has it all. But we must not be deceived.

Gospel in the Home

God's vision for our family is so much greater than all that we possess or achieve. We were made to project his image, his glory—not ours. In God's vision, parents hold a place of honor for a lifetime, and children show obedience and respect. In God's vision, parents nurture and train children to know Jesus. When we focus our family on this vision and live it out, we showcase the grace of the gospel in the home.

Father God,
Thank you for adopting us as your children, in Christ.
Thank you for your Word
that gives us nurture, discipline, and instruction
to navigate toward your best for us.
Forgive our pride.
We seek your glory, not our own.
Amen.

Six

FOR RICHER, FOR POORER

After watching a movie at home, it's interesting to watch the extras too. You get a behind-the-scenes look at how the movie was made, with some commentary from the director and the cast. They often freeze-frame a certain scene and provide insight you might have missed during the movie.

This chapter is like that.

We're going to freeze the frame.

We opened with the creation love story of Adam and Eve, who were created in the image of God and made for each other. Then the plot twisted as we watched their tragic fall from grace that left all of humanity broken and separated from God.

Enter redemption. In Christ, God offered a way to restore our brokenness. And, in God's design for the intimate relationship of husband and wife, we witnessed the love of Christ for the church. Then we talked about the joys and challenges of raising children.

All of these scenes bring to life the glory of the gospel in the home.

Now, let's go back to the scene where the bride and groom stand face-to-face to exchange wedding vows:

From this day forward,
For better, for worse,
For richer, for poorer . . .

Pause. Something here deserves an extra look.

For richer, for poorer.

When we say those words as bride and groom, we have no idea how much struggle we're going to encounter regarding money. But money has a way of causing stress in our lives—so much that it keeps many of us awake at night.

A recent poll found that two thirds of all Americans lose sleep regularly because of financial issues.[18] The poll was conducted by *Divorce Magazine,* which reports financial stress as the number-one cause of divorce today.

Other research indicates that one third of young Americans, between the ages of 25 and 29, cite financial concern as a reason to postpone or avoid marriage.[19]

And, did you know that more than 2,300 verses of Scripture deal with the subject of money? Jesus talked about money more than heaven and hell combined.

So it's clear that money matters—and not only in marriage. But since marriage is the most intimate human relationship entrusted to

---

18. http://www.usnews.com/news/articles/2015/06/25/more-than-three-fifths-of-americans-losing-sleep-over-finances

19. http://www.cheatsheet.com/business/a-nation-of-singles-fewer-americans-are-married-than-ever-before.html/?a=viewall

us, we'll use this context to explore how money affects us, for richer or for poorer.

Later in this chapter, we're going to bring our wives, Adrian and Mary, into the conversation. You've already met them briefly in some of the personal stories we have shared throughout the book. Soon, you'll get to hear from them directly as we discuss what we have learned about money in the context of our marriages.

Money Isn't the Problem

Wait a minute, you're thinking. You just said money is one of the most common causes of stress. And now you're saying money isn't the problem?

Yep.
Money matters, but it isn't the problem.
The problem is us.
Money is neutral. We're selfish.

The Bible says in 1 Timothy 6:10, "For the love of money is a root of all kinds of evils." People hear that and think money is evil. We think that because it's easier to blame money than to take a hard look at our hearts.

The rest of that verse says, "It is through this craving that some have wandered away from the faith and pierced themselves with many pangs." When we love money—when we crave it—that's the problem.

Some people think they would do better if they had more money. But even winning the lottery won't fix the root problem in the heart of humanity. Whether we're richer or poorer, we can become obsessed with money. Whether we're richer or poorer, we can use and chase after money for selfish purposes.

When our hearts go unchecked, we tend toward one of two extremes in response to money: worry or worship.

We worry whether we're richer or poorer. When we're richer, we worry about holding on to our money. When we're poorer, we worry about having enough.

In the same way, we can worship money, whether we're richer or poorer. When we're richer, we form unhealthy attachments to the pleasure and power that money affords us. When we're poorer, we may become jealous for what we don't have or make unwise spending choices to keep up appearances.

Which are you, a worrier or a worshiper? Take an honest look at yourself as we explore this subject.

This chapter will do more than give you money management tips. We'll provide some ideas, for sure. But the more important question we'll address is: How does the gospel transform the way we view and use our money?

We'll begin by turning in the Bible to the Sermon on the Mount, recorded in the gospel of Matthew, chapters 5 to 7. Crowds had gathered to hear Jesus. These days, this sermon would be one of the most shared podcasts ever.

In the Sermon on the Mount, Jesus reveals what righteousness in the kingdom of God looks like. And as we explore this sermon, we find two things that can transform our relationship with money.

First, we discover our need for the gospel, because Jesus raises the bar of righteousness so high that there's not enough religion on the planet to get us there. This is his intention. He wants us to see that the righteousness of the kingdom of God far exceeds any righteousness we might strive to accomplish on our own. We need the gospel. We need righteousness that comes from someone other than ourselves.

And second, we discover what a life transformed by the gospel looks like. It shows how we can rest in the righteousness of Christ, allowing him to transform who we are and how we live.

In this context, the Sermon on the Mount speaks to the way we handle money and possessions. It speaks to how we wrestle with worry and worship. Let's look specifically at Matthew 6:19 to 23:

For Richer, for Poorer

Do not lay up for yourselves treasures on earth, where moth and rust destroy and where thieves break in and steal, but lay up for yourselves treasures in heaven, where neither moth nor rust destroys and where thieves do not break in and steal. For where your treasure is, there your heart will be also.

Treasure. What a powerful word. More than simply describing the value of something, it reflects the place something holds in our hearts. Richer or poorer, we all have things we treasure.

The gospel empowers us to see the greater treasure.

Notice the warning in these words of Jesus: "Do not lay up for yourselves treasures on earth." When he says *lay up* or *store up*, he's referring to the things we pursue, consume, and accumulate. On earth, we seek these things for ourselves, our homes, and our perceived power and influence. Beyond simply meeting our needs, these things become our treasures.

Jesus makes a distinction here between two types of treasures: earthly and heavenly. He says that earthly treasures are vulnerable to *rust*. In the Greek language of New Testament manuscripts, the word is *brosis*, meaning "eating away at." Earthly treasures will decay.

The shine will wear off.
The paint will chip.
The new-car smell will disappear.
The house will get creaky.
The stock market will go down.
The economy will go south.

Because earthly treasures are unstable.
They're not trustworthy.

They're not secure.
They simply won't last.

Jesus teaches us to lay up treasures of a different kind—the blessings and rewards promised to those who are faithful to God's kingdom. Those treasures are eternal.

So how do we store up treasures that will last forever?

By stewarding your money and possessions as God-given resources.
By living to advance the gospel and the kingdom of God.
By giving generously.

When we do these things, when we live this way, the Bible says we're storing up treasures in heaven. With these treasures, we don't have to worry about what might wear off, wear down, or wear out. We won't be drawn to worship temporary pleasure and power.

Of the two treasures Jesus describes, heaven holds the greater treasure. When we recognize this truth, we understand why money isn't the problem. Instead, we must examine the desires of our hearts.

The Heart of the Matter

In whatever treasure we seek—earthly or heavenly—we will experience what Matthew 6:21 says: "For where your treasure is, there your heart will be also." So where is your treasure? Where do you find your worth? Where do you find your identity?

When Jesus talks about the heart, he's referring to the inner person—your will, your focus, your desires, and your emotions. He's pointing to the things you chase after, the things you long for, and he's saying that wherever you store up treasure, that's where your heart will be.

People sometimes get this backwards. They say that your treasure follows your heart, meaning that you'll store up whatever you truly love. But that's not what Jesus is saying here. He points to a danger that's the other way around: you'll grow to love what you store up.

There's a big difference here.
Don't miss it.
Your heart always follows your treasure.

You see, it's easy for us to store up things for all kinds of reasons—things we want, things we enjoy, things we think we're supposed to have. And then, over time, we grow to love those things too much to let them go. They become our security. They become our identity. They become our treasures. But are they earthly or heavenly treasures?

One Bible scholar says it this way: "We must store our wealth above in order that our hearts may be drawn upward. The two [money and heart] act and react upon one another."[20]

Maybe you've thought:
I wish I had more of a heart for the kingdom of God.
I wish I had a bigger heart for people who don't know Jesus.
I wish I felt a deeper connection to the church.

Guess what? You'll grow a bigger heart for those things as you begin to store up treasure in them. Invest yourself in them. Begin to use your time, money, and possessions to advance those things. This is a game-changer, because it's all about perspective. It's all about what you see as the greater treasure.

Your heart always follows your treasure.

Let's continue in Matthew 6:22 to 23. These are some of the most confusing verses in all of Scripture, and yet they are important to understand.

---

20. Alfred Plummer, *An Exegetical Commentary on the Gospel According to St. Matthew* (New York: Charles Scribner's Sons, 1910), 106.

The eye is the lamp of the body. So, if your eye is healthy, your whole body will be full of light, but if your eye is bad, your whole body will be full of darkness. If then the light in you is darkness, how great is the darkness!

The idea here is like double vision. You can't look at two things being equally focused on both at once. You can *see* both things, but you can only *focus* on one thing. The same is true of our hearts. We can't focus on two kinds of treasure. We must choose.

Just as your physical eyes determine the direction of your body, so your spiritual eyes determine the direction of your heart. What you see as most valuable will become the desire of your heart.

If you see earthly treasures as most valuable, then the direction and trajectory of your life will be to pursue those things—because, you've already heard it:

Your heart always follows your treasure.

But if you see the kingdom of heaven as a place where the greater treasure can be stored up, then the focus of your life will be in that direction. So, what do you see as the greater treasure? What are you pursuing? What are you storing up?

The gospel empowers us to serve the greater master.

As Jesus continues the Sermon on the Mount, he reinforces the double-vision idea in Matthew 6:24, which says:

No one can serve two masters, for either he will hate the one and love the other, or he will be devoted to the one and despise the other. You cannot serve God and money.

The word *serve* here is translated from a Greek word that literally means *bondservant* or *slave*. In the first-century Roman era when

Jesus was speaking, slaves were common. A slave could not serve two different masters with the same devotion to each.

Today, we might say we're masters of our own destiny. We're in charge. We can make our own decisions, thank you very much.

Not true.

We're all serving something or somebody.

We're either serving the things of this earth, or we're serving God's kingdom. Make no mistake. No one can serve two masters.

When we serve money and material possessions, when we give those things our greatest attention, we're serving that master. And this verse goes so far as to say, "either he will hate the one and love the other, or he will be devoted to the one and despise the other." When we serve money as the greater master, it's as if we hate and despise God's kingdom. That's strong language. We're either serving money as our god or we're serving God with our money.

For anyone who thinks, *Well, I struggle with a little greed; it's not a big deal,* Jesus would say that even a little greed is considered hatred toward God. He will not accept divided loyalty. Either you're all in, or you're not.

When you see money as *most valuable* instead of seeing money as *most usable for what is actually most valuable,* you're a slave to money. And money makes a horrible master.

Here's the great grace of God and the invitation of the gospel. We are invited, empowered and enabled to serve the greater master. Listen to 1 Timothy 6:17, where the apostle Paul writes:

As for the rich in this present age, charge them not to be haughty, nor to set their hopes on the uncertainty of riches, but on God, who richly provides us with everything to enjoy.

In developed countries like the United States, even the lowest economic position is wealthy compared to the majority of the world. Who are the rich in this present age? We are. Paul's words remind us not to put our hope in the uncertainty of money, because money makes a terrible ruler.

Money is a master that will always over-promise and under-deliver. *Always*. It'll never be able to pay out what we think it should. It will always fail us. It's here one day and it's gone the next.

But there's a greater master. Paul says to set our hopes on God, who richly provides us with everything to enjoy. Trust the Lord. Serve the Lord. Let him be the master of your life. And see what happens in verses 18 to 19:

> **They are to do good, to be rich in good works, to be generous and ready to share, thus storing up treasure for themselves as a good foundation for the future, so that they may take hold of that which is truly life.**

Did you catch that part about storing up treasure? Does that sound familiar? And here's the promise: *so that they may take hold of that which is truly life.*

That which is *truly* life.

Again, there's a big difference here between common thinking and what Jesus is actually saying—so don't miss it.

When you live under the mastery of money, you're missing out on that which is truly life. Sure, you might enjoy it. You might acquire some wonderful things. But ultimately, you'll miss the deep-down soul satisfaction of the life you were created for.

But when you leverage your life, serving the greater master—when you live generously, sharing your possessions with those in need and using your gifts to advance the kingdom of God—then you genuinely experience that which is truly life.

The reason so many unhappy people in the world are miserable isn't due to a lack of wealth. It's due to a lack of understanding that where your treasure is, there your heart will be also. People don't realize how to take hold of that which is is truly life.

So which master are you serving? Where do you find your treasure, your worth, and your identity? You cannot serve God and money.

Sometimes we affirm theological statements only to discover that what we really believe is revealed on our bank statements. Check yours.

Generosity is an outworking of the gospel. We are generous toward others because God was first generous toward us. We share because God has richly shared. We give because God so richly gave. God poured out his grace upon us, and we, in turn, become messengers of his grace to the world when we serve the greater master.

The gospel empowers us to seek first the greater kingdom.

In the Sermon on the Mount, we've just heard Jesus talk about laying up treasures in heaven. And we've heard his warning that we cannot serve both God and money. So what comes next? In Matthew 6:25 to 34, he immediately launches into a teaching on anxiety. We added italics to a few words to call them out as you read:

> *Therefore* I tell you, do not be *anxious* about your life, what you will eat or what you will drink, nor about your body, what you will put on. Is not life more than food, and the body more than clothing? Look at the birds of the air: they neither sow nor reap nor gather into barns, and yet your heavenly Father feeds them. Are you not of more value than they?
>
> And which of you by being *anxious* can add a single hour to his span of life? And why are you *anxious* about clothing? Consider the lilies of the field, how they grow: they neither toil nor spin, yet I tell you, even Solomon in all his glory was not arrayed like one of these. But if God so clothes the grass of the field, which

today is alive and tomorrow is thrown into the oven, will he not much more clothe you, O you of little faith?

Therefore do not be *anxious,* saying, 'What shall we eat?' or 'What shall we drink?' or 'What shall we wear?' For the Gentiles seek after all these things, and your heavenly Father knows that you need them all. But seek first the kingdom of God and his righteousness, and all these things will be added to you. *Therefore* do not be *anxious* about tomorrow, for tomorrow will be *anxious* for itself. Sufficient for the day is its own trouble.

Did you notice that Jesus used the word *anxious* six times? Did you also notice he said *therefore* three times? When you're studying the Bible and you see the word *therefore,* ask yourself *"What's it there for?"* It's always a word that connects two ideas. In this case, Jesus wants us to understand that our anxiety is often tied to financial stress.

He's essentially saying: *Therefore—in light of what I just told you about money—don't be anxious.* Then Jesus asks a series of questions. *Isn't there more to life than just consuming? More than what you eat and drink, what you wear, where you live?*

By asking us to examine our own hearts, he reminds us of a very important truth: There's more to life than all the things that the majority of us spend the better part of our lives focusing on—and therefore worrying about. See, the reality is this: Your heart always follows your treasure, and anxiety follows right along with it.

Do you have a tendency to worry about money? Most of us do.

Jesus says that our anxiety results from a lack of trust in the goodness of God. He uses two illustrations here: the birds of the air and the lilies of the field. They don't worry about what to eat or what to wear. They live by the provision God has given them. They showcase more color and beauty than the wealthy and wise King Solomon.

And then again, Jesus asks questions: *Are you not of more value than they?* The answer is *yes*. We were created in the image of God. If he provides for the rest of his creation, will he not also provide for us? The answer is *yes*.

And which of you by being anxious can add a single hour to his span of life? The answer is *none of us*. God alone gives us life and breath. If he sustains the rest of his creation, will he not also sustain us us? Again, the answer is *yes*.

At the root of worry is a lack of trust in the goodness of God.

In the time of Jesus, Gentiles were pagans who did not worship God—so of course, they did not trust in the goodness of God. They pursued earthly, perishable treasure. They focused on what to eat and what to wear. They worried about money and possessions.

Paul says in Ephesians 3:8 that he was sent "to preach to the Gentiles the unsearchable riches of Christ." Heavenly treasure.

The message to the Gentiles remains good news for us today. In light of the gospel, we no longer have to live in darkness or with double vision or under the thumb of the horrible master. We see the greater treasure, serve the greater master, and seek the greater kingdom.

And did you notice that Matthew 6:33 does not say, *seek the kingdom*. It says, seek *first* the kingdom. The Greek word here is *protos*, from which we get *priority*.

When it comes to money, we are to make heaven our priority.

Put heaven above everything else.

Above possessions.
Above giftedness.
Above ambition.
Above career.

Seek *first* the kingdom of God. This is how to determine the direction of your life and family and work—and it applies to money. In this context of the Sermon on the Mount, Jesus is speaking primarily about money. He says to seek God's kingdom above everything else. And when you do, your handling of money and your freedom of anxiety will make it evident that you are making God's kingdom your priority.

This approach to money isn't something you work into your life; it will take top priority of your life.

But practically speaking, what does it look like? And in particular, what does that look like in marriage? The best way we know to answer these questions is to let you in on a conversation that includes our wives, Adrian and Mary.

As married couples, we said our vows—for richer, for poorer—and then we began to learn from experience what those vows require of us. We'll share with you what we've discovered, sometimes the hard way—because we're as broken as anybody. But we're committed to the covenant of marriage and to seeking first the kingdom of God in stewardship of everything he has entrusted to us.

• • •

Connor: For Mary and me, there have been seasons in our marriage when money has truly been a struggle for us. I tend to be the one who worries about money. Worry shows up when I don't think we have enough or when I think we've spent too much.

Mary: I would say that I have worshiped money. I have been a frivolous spender. I have found security in money, and I have not always been a good steward.

Todd: Early in our marriage, Adrian and I failed in the area of finances. We went through six or seven years of arguing, fighting, stressing, worrying, and not managing well. In our house, I'm a worshiper of money. I enjoy spending it a little too much. But Adrian is . . .

For Richer, for Poorer

Adrian: I'm a worrywart.

Todd: But eventually, we discovered several principles that transformed our marriage and how we handle money. I hope that talking about these will be an encouragement to you.

Connor: So often, there are two responses toward money: worry and worship. Now that we can look back on it, I like to tease Mary about spending $180 on candles at Pottery Barn—within our first month of marriage. Come on! Candles?

Mary: Y'all, our apartment looked so cute, and it smelled so good. We probably still have some of those candles today.

Connor: I promise you we do. And fortunately, like Todd and Adrian, Mary and I also learned some biblical principles for how we handle money. You won't find these in a book—well, except this one. We developed this list ourselves.

1. The principle of stewardship: God owns everything, and we're responsible to manage what he entrusts to us.

Mary: First, we acknowledge that everything belongs to God, and when we give, we're actually returning to him what is already his. The Lord has been so faithful with us. He has taken us through so many seasons financially—seasons of struggle and seasons of change.

When we give our tithes and offerings back to the Lord, we are being obedient to what he has called us to do. It is not contingent on how much we have. We are called to steward his resources. As part of that stewardship, we are called to give back what is his.

Connor: Psalm 24:1 says, "The earth is the Lord's and the fullness thereof, the world and those who dwell therein." He owns the cattle on a thousand hills. If he needed something, he wouldn't ask us, because it's all his. When we acknowledge that it is his, and that he has entrusted it to us for a season, that puts us in the right position to tithe and to give sacrificially and generously.

Todd: This principle has transformed our lives too.

Adrian: After we understood that everything we have belongs to the Lord, we began to understand that whatever he has given us is exactly what he intended for us. This changed our mindset toward our finances, so we said: *Okay, this is what he has entrusted us with. What are we going to do with it? How are we going to be good stewards?*

We decided three things—that we would create a plan, be committed to it, and communicate often about it.

2. The principle of a spending plan: Create it, commit to it, and communicate about it often.

Connor: In our marriage, Mary and I reached the same decision to develop a budget, stick to it, and make sure we talk about it.

Early in our relationship, I was lazy about leadership in this area. I didn't sit down and develop a healthy spending plan, because I was fearful of what putting it on paper would actually say about my priorities.

I've heard it said, and I agree: *Either you tell your money where to go, or your money will tell you where it went.*

Todd: I didn't lead well in this area either. I thought my responsibility was to bring home the paycheck. Adrian is very administrative, so I figured she would pay the bills, and it would all work out in the end. But it didn't.

Then I became frustrated with Adrian and with our situation because I felt like a failure—like I wasn't providing enough money. But the real issue was money management.

Adrian: And since I'm a worrywart, I was consumed by anxiety about our finances. Yet, I tried to keep things hidden from Todd because I didn't want him to get upset. That ended up causing serious friction in our home, to the point I would go to sleep thinking about it—then I would wake up thinking about it. I felt alone and frustrated.

When we finally decided to develop a plan, it changed everything. Through prayer and communication and probably a good two weeks of working together, we determined every single line of our budget.

Todd: We prayed: *God, what are the goals you have for us? How do you want us to give? What are the things you want? How can we reorder our lifestyle in order to honor you with every penny we have?*

Adrian: We committed to each other that we would stick to our budget; we would not waver from it. We view our plan as the foundation of our finances.

Todd: When something unexpected comes up—maybe a doctor's visit or a bill we weren't planning on, we talk about it. We work through the options and develop a strategy to resolve that issue together.

Overall, we sit down to review our budget every three to six months. We'll evaluate our spending. We'll make sure we're on track. And we find ways to save money and realign our budget if we need to improve our cash flow. As a result, we discover new and creative ways to be better stewards. Our spending plan has been a game changer in every area of our relationship, because now we're on the same page in all the decisions related to it.

Adrian is still administrative. She's great at paying bills, writing checks, and making sure money is moving in the right direction. The process works because we've developed a plan together.

Connor: Todd and Adrian's experience reinforces the fact that anything worth having is worth working for. Like them, Mary and I have to be diligent and disciplined about it. We have to talk about it, even though it can be an awkward subject.

It's not like this is setting the table for romance, but Mary and I try to have money dates occasionally. Maybe we will go out to dinner, or we will put the kids to bed early so we can sit down and review things together. We will ask ourselves: *Are we meeting our goals? Are we putting money where we said we were going to put it?* This is a healthy thing to do, according to what the Scriptures teach us about stewardship of our resources.

3. The principle of enough: Spend wisely and save reasonably.

Todd: Once we had a budget in place, with commitment and communication, we had a way to become wise spenders and reasonable savers.

Connor: Or as we like to say: Be savers, not hoarders.

Mary: And also: Be a *steward*, not *stupid*.

Todd: What we're getting at is this: Understand what enough is. Just because you *can* doesn't mean you *should*. For example, when you get a raise, what happens? Does it disappear before you know it? Sometimes, people plan ahead how they want to spend a raise before it even comes. But just because have money to spend doesn't mean you should spend it.

Connor: And likewise, just because you can *save* money doesn't mean you should. Now, don't take this the wrong way. Life insurance is good. Saving for college is good. Saving toward retirement is wise. In the book of Proverbs, we see over and over again the wisdom of saving and good stewardship.

But saving is not an excuse for greed; saving is not hoarding. God has entrusted us with resources, in part, to bless us with the ability to be generous toward others. Are you hoarding when you should be sharing? Think about that.

Mary: As I mentioned earlier, I didn't exercise a lot of wisdom around spending when Connor and I were first married. That not only caused strain in our relationship, but it also limited how generous we could be. I always wanted us to be the people who would help others if a need came up. But because I had not been wise, we were not in a position to give generously.

The Lord was faithful to call me out on that, and he had us do some really hard things. He had us sell a house that we had bought only six months earlier to be our "forever home." We had big plans, and we had spent money on those plans. Then God quickly and clearly told us to sell that house. We needed to get out of debt. So we moved into an apartment with two small children.

That was when Connor was called into ministry, and we thought the Lord was preparing us to make a transition. What we didn't know was that a few months after we got out of debt, we would have our third child—a daughter with severe special needs. She needed multiple surgeries, and you know what? We were able to pay for all of her medical expenses because the Lord had gotten ahold of our finances.

I'm not saying the Lord is going to bless you abundantly with money if you're obedient, but I do think he is faithful. He always provides, even if we don't know what that's going to look like.

Todd: Here's another thing to think about in terms of spending wisely and saving reasonably: Just because you *don't* want to do something doesn't mean you shouldn't.

There are some things God has told us we need to do. Live generously. Tithe. Invest in family time. But sometimes we get stingy, and we don't want to spend money on anything.

Spending wisely might mean you *should* go on that trip—a

reasonable trip—because you're investing in relationships. So talk about that. Make sure you're saving enough but also spending enough to fulfill God's vision for your family.

Adrian: As a mom, I've just decided I was going to lead the charge in this area for our household. I want to be a saver, and I want to spend our money wisely. So, for example, when I go to the grocery store, it's very planned. I do not walk in the grocery store and just have at it, because it will end badly. And, when our kids need clothes, they don't need everything brand name.

Todd: When you spoil your kids by giving them too much, especially at a young age, they develop a mindset: *Life is about me.* But when you have conversations with them, and you say, *We could buy that, but we're not going to because we have these priorities,* then you're teaching your kids to seek first the kingdom of God. They learn that life is not about them and what they want.

Adrian: Through these kinds of decisions, we've taught our kids about stewardship. They are actually taking part in it, and it has been a neat journey to see them starting to understand it. Yes, we could spend a lot more money on food and clothes, but we're choosing not to—and that allows us to give more to the Lord, which is our goal.

Todd: When it comes to saving, we advise everyone to have a savings account. Even if you can only set aside a small amount on a regular basis, set up an account for that.

Some people wrongly think that a savings account shows a lack of faith that God will provide. In fact, the opposite is true: Your savings is God's provision today for tomorrow. This is not about finding your security in a big bank account. But do save, and be reasonable about it.

4. The principle of generosity: Since God owns everything, live with open hands.

Connor: Mary and I talk about what it means to grow in sharing, not just storing. As I said earlier, greed has no place in the kingdom of God. We are called to be generous people, to live with open hands.

Dave Ramsey says to live like no one else, so you can give like no one else. It's countercultural to live below your means. It's countercultural to live on less. But that's where generosity begins.

Todd: We're back to where we started this chapter, with the words of Jesus in the Sermon on the Mount: "For where your treasure is, there your heart will be also."

I encourage people to start with the tithe because I believe the Bible sets a pattern for us in the Old Testament. God wants to teach his people generosity, so he gave the instruction to tithe.

Tithe simply means *one tenth*. So, you take one tenth of what God has entrusted to you—your income—and you give it to the work of the kingdom of God. Another biblical word for this is *firstfruits*. In an agricultural context, families would literally give the first portion of whatever they harvested.

Adrian: In our home, I was the guilty party when it came to tithing. I did not understand the tithe. I did not feel the need to tithe, so I showed a lot of resistance during the early years of our marriage.

Todd helped me come to the realization that generosity does not mean leftovers. It's not about having some extra money and thinking, *Oh, we're going to be generous and give it to the church this month.*

The Lord really shifted my focus to what the tithe is—which is sacrificial giving. So we rearranged our lives. We rearranged our home and our lifestyle so that we were giving a tithe regularly.

Ann Voskamp expresses this principle so well:

We're not giving what we're called to give, unless that giving affects how we live—affects what we put on our plate and where we make our home and hang our hat and what kind of threads we've got to have on our back.

Surplus Giving is the leftover you can afford to give; Sacrificial Giving is the love gift that changes how you live—because the love of Christ has changed you. God doesn't want your leftovers. God wants your love overtures, your first-overs, because He is your first love. [21]

Our tithe is the first check I write every single month. It is the top priority on our list. In addition to our tithe, there are many ways God has blessed us to give above and beyond and to get our family involved in learning what it means to be generous.

Todd: The discipline of tithing was a game changer for us. It had been an area of unfaithfulness for a long time. But now we have learned that this is how we seek first the kingdom of God.

Connor: If this is an area where you need to grow, then we're not judging you. If you've never developed a spending plan, if you've not learned the balance of spending and saving, if you've not been faithful in tithing and being generous—start today.

Todd and Adrian, Mary and I—we didn't start out our marriages with a biblical foundation for how we would handle our money. But when we recognized the need, we did something about it. So, do something today. A lot of local churches offer classes and counseling on financial management. Sign up. Get going. Make the choice to honor God with your finances.

---

21. http://www.aholyexperience.com/2014/10/what-the-north-american-church-is-the-most-hungry-for/

For Richer, for Poorer

Todd: Absolutely. I would give the same challenge to everyone—and not only because God has entrusted you with the responsibility of stewardship. But also because it's one of the best things you can do for the health of your marriage. Too many marriages falter and fail because of financial stress. Don't let yours be one of them. Especially when you have the opportunity to take hold of that which is truly life.

So, have the hard conversations you need to have with your spouse. Look at your income. Look at your spending. Look at your saving and your giving. For richer, for poorer, make the commitment together to:

See the greater treasure.

Serve the greater master.

Seek first the greater kingdom.

Lord Jesus,
Make your words a reality in our hearts,
that we would seek first the kingdom of God—
the same God who owns everything
and has entrusted us with all that we have.
We are grateful.
Now help us be wise and generous.
Amen.

Seven

A SINGLE PURPOSE

Posting a single relationship status has become a joke to a lot of people on social media. You know . . .

Waiting for a miracle.
On a pint-sized 'date' with Ben and Jerry.
That moment when your friends find out Jamie is your cat.
Independently owned and operated.

Even when you're in a relationship, everybody knows that becoming "Facebook official" brings the risk of embarrassment later on if things don't work out. Break-ups are more public, and therefore more painful.

You're constantly aware of your online profile and photos—not to mention whatever your friends have tagged about you. There's a lot of pressure to manage the image you present to the world. *It's complicated.* Most definitely.

And underneath it all, there's a simple truth: We all long to be loved.

When it comes to finding a soul mate, we're looking for someone who will change our life, not just our relationship status.

You likely picked up this book in the first place because you're in a relationship, or you have been. Maybe it's a serious dating relationship. Maybe you're married. Or perhaps you've broken up with someone.

Regardless of your relationship status, this chapter offers principles for future fulfillment as the person God made you to be. But be clear about one thing: If you're looking for fulfillment in another person, you'll be disappointed. Don't set yourself up for that.

Keep reading, and you'll discover why and how to live with a single purpose that resonates with the grace of the gospel.

• • •

Social media humor highlights the stigma that often comes with being single in our culture. The crazy number of Internet dating sites and TV shows like *The Bachelor* only reinforce the idea that singleness is supposed to be temporary.

As if singleness is second-rate.

As if solo life is somehow insufficient.

As if you're nobody without somebody.

Those are lies. All lies.

So it's a loaded question when someone asks, *Are you dating anyone?* When you're unattached, the curiosity of friends or family can imply an expectation: *Hurry up and find someone.* Maybe even at church, people with good intentions can't wait for you to get a sweetheart and get married. You feel more like a project than a person.

But when you're in a great relationship, people hardly have to ask. You're grateful to have found someone—and who wouldn't be? You love talking about your love.

As if things couldn't be better.

A Single Purpose

As if you'll live happily ever after.
As if your life is now complete.

But be careful—because those are lies too.

We need a biblical perspective of both singleness and marriage. We need to recognize the gift and the grace God gives us in every season of life. His purpose for us is much more significant than a relationship status.

So we're going to turn once again to the words of Scripture, written by the apostle Paul. When it comes to certain relationship questions, we can learn a lot from 1 Corinthians 7—which you may want to read entirely before we continue. It will take you about five minutes. Throughout this chapter, we will be referring to various verses from this passage. Be prepared for some strange verses; we'll be sure to explain them as we go along.

Paul is writing to a young church in Corinth—an ancient Greek city known for its culture and commerce. Corinth had quite a reputation for promiscuous sex. In the context of 1 Corinthians 7, you can tell that Paul is helping the Corinthian church navigate questions that have come up about sex, morality, marriage, and singleness.

And for Paul, the answers all come down to purpose—a single purpose rooted in the sovereignty of God and lived out in Christ-centered relationships.

Living with a single purpose means trusting God as sovereign over every season.

What season of life are you in? Are you single? Married? Divorced? Do you want kids? Do you have kids? Are you restless or grateful? Are you worried or hopeful?

Regardless of what season you're in, you'll gain perspective when you recognize that God is in control. In 1 Corinthians 7:17, Paul says:

Only let each person lead the life that the Lord has assigned to him, and to which God has called him.

Your life is not by accident. God knows exactly who you are and where you are. He created you in his image. He called you according to his purpose. He knows exactly what season you're in—and he's right here with you.

God is *sovereign*. That's not a word we use much these days. It means to have supreme or ultimate power. It means God is in control. No matter whether you're in a terrific or terrible season, let God's sovereignty be a source of confidence and comfort to you. God is in control.

Now, this doesn't mean you can blame God for the consequences of your choices. God's sovereignty doesn't eliminate your responsibility. So there's no excuse for making bad choices because you're in a bad season. You're still called to follow him in obedience and trust.

Back in the book of Genesis, several chapters after the story of Adam and Eve, we meet Abraham and Sarah. In Genesis 12:1 to 3, we read an incredible promise from God—a promise that reaches far beyond a season of life to become a legacy. The Lord said to Abraham:

> **"Go from your country and your kindred and your father's house to the land that I will show you. And I will make of you a great nation, and I will bless you and make your name great, so that you will be a blessing. I will bless those who bless you, and him who dishonors you I will curse, and in you all the families of the earth shall be blessed."**

God is saying, *I have great plans for you.* A great nation means a great number of descendants—a great number of families. In the time of Abraham and Sarah, this is a tremendous honor.

Only one small problem: They are well past their childbearing years, and they have no children. So where exactly is this great nation going to come from?

A Single Purpose

God, are you sure you've got this?

Years passed, and still no children for Abraham and Sarah.

Abraham and Sarah get restless. So what do they do? They decide God needs some help to get this promise going. They take matters into their own hands.

Following an ancient custom, Abraham goes to his servant Hagar and sleeps with her, and has a son. But that was not God's purpose or promise for Abraham. And let's just say that things do not go well between Sarah and Hagar after that.

Eventually, despite their old age, Abraham and Sarah conceive and give birth to a son—a fulfillment of God's promise. Despite their lack of trust, God proves his sovereignty by accomplishing what seemed humanly impossible.

And to this day, God is still sovereign. He is sovereign over the season you're in. He has a purpose for your life. You may not be able to see it right now, but trust that God is in control.

• • •

In our culture, single people can be fooled into thinking that finding a soul mate is God's purpose for them. A soul mate is a wonderful gift, for sure—although perhaps not God's purpose for you in this season. Or, if you have found a husband or wife, you might think you're all set.

But the point is not about *singleness*, it's about *sovereignty*. That's why this chapter applies to everyone, regardless of relationship status.

You may be single.
You may be in a serious relationship.
You may be married.
You may have lost your spouse to death or divorce.

Whatever the season, God is in control.

At this point, we do want to say a few things especially for those who are not married—because that was Paul's reality as he wrote to the church in Corinth. He was not married. In I Corinthians 7:6 to 9 he says:

> **Now as a concession, not a command, I say this. I wish that all were as I myself am. But each has his own gift from God, one of one kind and one of another.**
>
> **To the unmarried and the widows I say that it is good for them to remain single as I am. But if they cannot exercise self-control, they should marry. For it is better to marry than to burn with passion.**

Paul is not against marriage. Just the opposite. He holds marriage and family in high regard. Earlier in this book, we explored some of Paul's teaching on marriage from Ephesians 5. We saw how he paints the portrait of love between husband and wife like that between Christ and the church—an illustration of the gospel in the home.

So no, Paul is not opposed to marriage. He affirms it as a gift from God. At the same time, he says that singleness is a gift from God too. *Each has his own gift from God, one of one kind and one of another.*

The word *gift* here is interesting, because it comes from the Greek word *charisma*. It's the idea of spiritual giftedness. It's supernatural. And the word *each* means literally each person—including you, regardless of your relationship status. You have been given a spiritual gift from God, so embrace it—embrace who you are in this season.

Not some future version of you.
Not you 15 pounds lighter.
Not you after grad school.

Not you after the wedding.
Not you after the baby is born.
Not you after saving enough money to buy a house.
Not you after getting the new job you interviewed for.
Not you after you get through this season.

But right now, in this season. Live today in the power of the Holy Spirit. Lead the life the Lord has called you to. Trust his sovereignty. And in doing so, you will reflect his image in you, his glory through you.

Connor: The Moment Right In Front of Us

Last year, my family went to Houston to see my in-laws at Thanksgiving. While we were there, I took my big kids and my father-in-law downtown for the Thanksgiving Day parade. We got there a little late, but we tried to find a spot where the kids could see the floats as the parade passed by.

I noticed others scurrying around and trying to position themselves to see one certain float or another. They were constantly moving back and forth from one vantage point to another, trying to get a better view.

Meanwhile, the floats passed by.

For some of us, that's how we treat the season God has called us to. If we would just stay put, we would see and experience whatever he is passing before us. But often we're scurrying around, trying to get into the position we think is best for us.

Ultimately, it's exhausting. And we end up missing the parade—the joy of the moment passing right in front of us.

Living with a single purpose means finding your identity and fulfillment in Christ.

When we understand that every season of life rests on God's sovereignty, we can trust his purpose for us. This is hugely important. It means we can be set free from worrying about our relationship status. Instead, we can choose to focus on our identity in Christ.

Now contrast that with how we can get caught up in crafting our image on social media—how carefully we talk about our lives. In every post, we are saying, *This is who I am.*

> Married or unmarried.
> Dating or not dating.
> Graduated from this school.
> Working at this job.
> Sharing photos that make me look cool or adventurous or funny or whatever I want to be known for.

This is life—and of course, we want to be honest about life. But if we're not careful, we start to attach our identity to our earthly status. We risk losing sight of our true identity, rooted in our relationship with Jesus Christ. When it comes to our relationship status in particular, we risk losing sight of the purpose and potential that comes with finding our fulfillment in him.

Gary Thomas, the author of numerous books on marriage and spiritual life, points to the core of our identity when he says:

> **Marriage doesn't solve emptiness; it exposes it. . . . If someone can't live without you, he or she will never be happy living with you either.**[22]

---

22. Gary Thomas, *Sacred Search*, (Colorado Springs, CO: David C. Cook, 2013), 209.

A Single Purpose

In other words, this isn't about anyone else. It's about you. It's between you and God.

In 1 Corinthians 7:24, Paul writes: "So, brothers, in whatever condition each was called, there let him remain with God." It doesn't say, *Remain with friends.* It doesn't say, *Remain with parents.* And no, it doesn't say to remain with your boyfriend or girlfriend, husband or wife.

Remain with God.

God is your divine companion.

We jumped into verse 24 without taking a look at the preceding verses, which help us understand even more of what Paul is talking about.

Before we read the preceding verses, you need to know that Paul refers to circumcision and uncircumcision to indicate ethnic and religious identity. This is not simply a question of a medical procedure on a baby boy. By tradition, Jews practice circumcision as a sign of identity within a covenant community.

Look at the context of verses 18 to 24:

> **Was anyone at the time of his call already circumcised? Let him not seek to remove the marks of circumcision. Was anyone at the time of his call uncircumcised? Let him not seek circumcision. For neither circumcision counts for anything nor uncircumcision, but keeping the commandments of God. Each one should remain in the condition in which he was called.**

> **Were you a bondservant when called? Do not be concerned about it. (But if you can gain your freedom, avail yourself of the opportunity.) For he who was called in the Lord as a bondservant is a freedman of the Lord. Likewise he who was free when called is a bondservant of Christ. You were bought with a price; do not become bondservants of men.**

So, brothers, in whatever condition each was called, there let him remain with God.

Whoa. There's a lot to explain here. You're probably wondering, *What in the world is he talking about?*

Paul is still talking about singleness and marriage. He's making a comparison to circumcision and uncircumcision, and to slavery and freedom.

Now you're thinking: *This just got really weird. What does slavery have to do with this?*

Hang in there. The point is about identity.

1. Your identity is rooted in Christ. In Paul's day, people were identified as Jewish or Greek—circumcised or uncircumcised. They were also identified as slave or free. This is not an endorsement of slavery; it's simply a reference to first-century Roman reality—and it's the beginning of how the gospel proclaims freedom for all people.

Paul is saying that identity in Christ trumps everything. It trumps whether you're Jewish or Greek. It trumps whether you're slave or free. And it trumps whether you're single or married.

Your identity in Christ is not tied to your ethnic, economic, or relationship status. He loves you. He redeems you. That's what matters most. Period.

Does marriage shape things about a person? Of course. Does singleness shape things about a person? Absolutely. Marriage is great, but it's not your identity.

In Galatians 3:27 to 28, Paul expressed a similar thought more simply:

For as many of you as were baptized into Christ have put on Christ. There is neither Jew nor Greek, there is neither slave nor free, there is no male and female, for you are all one in Christ Jesus.

A Single Purpose

This is a great the beauty of the gospel—a covenant community of relationships that go far beyond any earthly status we might have or pursue or obtain.

2. You are complete in Christ. Maybe you're thinking: *Sure, my identity is in Christ. But I feel incomplete when I'm not in a relationship. After all, God said it wasn't good for Adam to be alone.*

You're right. God created Eve for companionship with Adam. But we've seen in earlier chapters of this book how the Fall fractured the intimacy of God's design for marriage. We now live with the fallout from the Fall. And only in Christ can we be restored.

If you're looking for marriage to complete you, you're going to crush your spouse under the weight of unrealistic expectations—because you're looking to marriage to do for you what Christ has already done.

You are restored to wholeness in him.
You are complete in him.

Pastor and author J.D. Greear says the number-one singleness myth is that marriage equals completion. It's like that line from *Jerry Maguire* again: "You complete me." It's a great line for the movies, but it doesn't hold true in real life.[23]

There's nothing wrong with wanting to be married and enjoying marriage. And there's nothing wrong with desiring to have a family. These are gifts to be grateful for. But in Colossians 2:10 , Paul affirms: "and you have been filled in him, who is the head of all rule and authority."

---

23. http://www.jdgreear.com/my_weblog/2015/05/singleness-myth-2-you-need-to-find-the-right-person.html

Todd: Worth the Wait

As I mentioned back in the first chapter, I was the guy who wanted to get married as soon as possible. I couldn't wait to find Mrs. Right and live my dream of marrying young and starting a family.

Well, at the end of my senior year in high school I found *the one!* She was sweet, kind, and godly—the perfect fit for me. I was convinced that God intended us share the rest of our lives together. *It's going be awesome,* I told myself.

As our relationship progressed, we ended up choosing the same college. Again, a perfect fit. I imagined we would marry soon after.

All the while, I was driven by a genuine sense of longing—a reflection of God's design for companionship. I really believe that.

But as we began our freshman year at college, she had a change of heart. I was absolutely devastated. *God, how could this be? We both love you. I thought we loved each other. What's going on?*

I came to realize that I had put my hope in marriage. I was looking for a wife to complete me—to provide fulfillment that only Jesus can provide. But God knew my heart. He also knew my heartache. He was sovereign in that season as he is in every season. I needed to learn to put my hope in him. I needed to recognize that I am complete in Christ.

A few years later, I met a beautiful woman named Adrian. The rest is history. We have now celebrated 15 years together and have three amazing children. God granted that desire for me, and I'm incredibly grateful. It has been worth the wait—not only for my marriage and my family, but also for my calling and my relationship with Christ.

3. All your relationships in Christ will last forever. If you're living in a solo season—maybe you've never married, or you've been widowed or divorced—you may be asking: *What about companionship?*

God has wired us for relationships. It's part of our design as human beings. We want to share life in relationships. We still hear the echo from Genesis that it's not good to be alone.

But marriage is not God's only provision for companionship. It is *one* of God's provisions, but it's not the most lasting provision for our companionship. Even the covenant of marriage is temporary. It's a fleeting illustration of a much greater spiritual reality.

In Mark 12:18 to 25 Jesus says there is no marriage in heaven. Why? Because what marriage represents—the union of Christ and his church—becomes reality in heaven. We will no longer need the picture of earthly marriage.

This is not about lowering the view of marriage, which is a tremendous gift. But rather, it's about recognizing the deep and lasting relationships we find in the body of Christ.

Jesus teaches this in Matthew 12:46 to 50. Here's the story:

> **While he was still speaking to the people, behold, his mother and his brothers stood outside, asking to speak to him. But he replied to the man who told him, "Who is my mother, and who are my brothers?" And stretching out his hand toward his disciples, he said, "Here are my mother and my brothers! For whoever does the will of my Father in heaven is my brother and sister and mother."**

What is Jesus saying here? There is a companionship and a connection that runs deeper even than familial relationships.

John Piper explains it this way:

> **Jesus is turning everything around. Yes, he loved his mother and his brothers. But those are all natural and temporary**

relationships. . . . He came into the world to call out a people for his name from all families of the earth into a new family where single people in Christ are full-fledged family members on a par with all others, bearing fruit for God and becoming mothers and fathers of the eternal kind.[24]

Relationships in Christ are permanent and precious—more so than relationships in our earthly families. Our yearning for companionship is a God-given desire that even marriage cannot satisfy.

And what about children? Same thing. But God calls us to nurture spiritual offspring regardless of whether we have biological or adopted children. He gives us all kinds of spiritual children to mentor and disciple in the faith.

Think about the apostle Paul. The Bible names many of his spiritual offspring, but no earthly children. When you read Paul's various letters, he mentions men like Timothy and Titus, and women like Damaris and Lydia, and countless others. Spiritually speaking, they are Paul's descendants, and so are we.

In Christ, we discover our identity as men and women who are loved and redeemed by God. And we experience deep and lasting companionship with others who share our spiritual identity.

Living with a single purpose means committing yourself to the present in light of the future.

From the vantage point of the present season, what's next? Where do we go from here? As we continue reading 1 Corinthians 7, Paul encourages us to live today with forever in view. He says in verses 25 to 31:

---

24. http://www.desiringgod.org/messages/single-in-christ-a-name-better-than-sons-and-daughters

A Single Purpose

> Now concerning the betrothed, I have no command from the Lord, but I give my judgment as one who by the Lord's mercy is trustworthy. I think that in view of the present distress it is good for a person to remain as he is. Are you bound to a wife? Do not seek to be free. Are you free from a wife? Do not seek a wife. But if you do marry, you have not sinned, and if a betrothed woman marries, she has not sinned. Yet those who marry will have worldly troubles, and I would spare you that.
>
> This is what I mean, brothers: the appointed time has grown very short. From now on, let those who have wives live as though they had none, and those who mourn as though they were not mourning, and those who rejoice as though they were not rejoicing, and those who buy as though they had no goods, and those who deal with the world as though they had no dealings with it. For the present form of this world is passing away.

Paul is urging us not to trade the temporal for the eternal. Live in the present, but keep an eye on the future. He cautions us that *the present form of this world is passing away.*

When you're young and it feels like your whole life is ahead of you, it can be hard to accept the idea that everything in this world is temporary. You're trying to build something—your career, your relationships, your home.

But Paul is using exaggeration to make a point: Act as if none of this is relevant. He's not actually saying to abandon your responsibilities. He wants followers of Christ to recognize the urgency of eternity and commit to the cause of the gospel.

Your purpose, regardless of your relationship status, is to commit yourself to the cause of the gospel.

• • •

In earlier chapters of this book, we addressed what it looks like for married couples to dedicate themselves to the gospel in the home. So we're going to spend a little time to address what that looks like for individuals.

Maybe you are single, or you have friends who are. Or perhaps you'll draw insight here for raising a son or daughter with a biblical perspective on singleness.

Those who desire to be married are right to do that—just not at the expense of their calling to follow and serve Christ. So, let's look at three priorities for living in the present season while keeping eternity in focus.

1. Pursue a Christ-centered dating relationship. A few pages back, we talked about the eternal value of relationships in Christ. Pursue them. This is crucial for friendship and dating. Seek the company of Jesus-professing, Bible-believing, God-fearing men and women. Seek those who display obvious signs of an ongoing and growing relationship with Christ.

If you're wondering whether or not to date someone, imagine that you're running a race. Run hard and fast toward Christ. That's your calling. That's your purpose. And if you look up and there is someone on your right or left who is likewise running hard and fast toward Christ, then that individual is worthy of your consideration for dating.

And let's be honest: You don't have to go on three dates to figure this out. You can tell within three hours—or less.

If you're dating someone, and Christ is not the love of their life, you know it. Don't stay in that relationship. Break it off now.

But maybe you're thinking, *I really love him.* Or, *I really care for her.* That's human nature. But we're talking here about a deeper, spiritual bond. Be sure that Christ has their heart before you give them yours.

2. Pursue integrity and purity as cornerstones of your relationship. If you have to tell lies to maintain a relationship, it's unhealthy. If

A Single Purpose

you're keeping up appearances so that your sweetheart or your friends or your parents will think something other than the truth—then you're dishonoring the integrity of your relationship.

If you're looking at stuff you shouldn't, if you're entertaining thoughts you shouldn't, if you're carrying on other intimate relationships—then purity is not your cornerstone.

Without integrity and purity, the foundation of your relationship will crumble—even if both of you love Christ.

But there's good news in the gospel: You can find forgiveness. You can work to repair and restore your relationship. But you've got to come clean. You've got to be honest. And you've got to make a commitment *together* to integrity and purity.

3. Pursue sanctification, not marriage preparation. It's a noble idea to think that being single is a season of preparation for marriage and family life. It sounds good on the surface, but it's misguided—because we're not preparing for something earthly. We're preparing for something heavenly.

Invest your life in sanctification, not marriage preparation. The goal is Christ, not your spouse. If marriage is a temporary picture of the gospel, then there's something more important than marriage—which is union with Christ.

So pursue holiness. Pursue Christ-likeness. Pursue real manhood and real womanhood. And when you do, you'll become ready for marriage at whatever time you may find your future husband or wife.

Commit to living for Christ today and keeping forever in view.

> ### Living with a single purpose means stewarding your life to serve God's kingdom.

When you pursue sanctification and Christ-likeness, you're going to find your attention drawn to serving God's kingdom. This is true whether you're married or single.

As we continue reading in 1 Corinthians 7:32 to 35, Paul explains certain advantages of being single:

> I want you to be free from anxieties. The unmarried man is anxious about the things of the Lord, how to please the Lord. But the married man is anxious about worldly things, how to please his wife, and his interests are divided.
>
> And the unmarried or betrothed woman is anxious about the things of the Lord, how to be holy in body and spirit. But the married woman is anxious about worldly things, how to please her husband. I say this for your own benefit, not to lay any restraint upon you, but to promote good order and to secure your undivided devotion to the Lord.

Paul is saying here what married couples know to be true: Sometimes marriage is worrisome. Healthy marriages require time, energy, and attention. So do children. Being unattached has advantages.

Let's put it this way. Surely you have thought back to a previous season in life and said to yourself or to a friend: *Life was simpler then. Things were easier then.* This is true of many married couples who look back on single life. And this is Paul's point.

When you're unmarried, and when you don't have children, you have flexibility that married couples and families simply don't have. You have a freedom to think about and serve God's kingdom more than anything else.

As pastors who are writing this book, we experience what this means in our own lives. We have to say *no* to certain opportunities in ministry for the sake of our families. This is not wrong—in fact, it's honorable within the covenant of marriage. But it's a reality. Our time is divided. Our finances are divided. Our attention is divided. The expression of our spiritual gifts is divided.

As married couples, we must steward our lives too, but it's going to look different for us.

A Single Purpose

Whether you are single or married, whether you're a parent or not, it's important to seize every season, every day. Make the most of your advantages. Make the most of glorifying God wherever you are.

If you're not doing that as a single person . . .
If you're not doing that as husband and wife . . .
If you're not doing that as a parent . . .
If you're not doing that as a follower of Christ . . .
. . . then what are you doing with your life?

Let's look at practical ways we can be good stewards. And here again, we're going to give emphasis to opportunities for those who are single to leverage this season of life.

1. Serve others and your church often. You have capacity and bandwidth to do a lot during a single season of life. Raise up spiritual children—meaning those who are young in the faith. Become a friend who can guide them in their journeys with Christ.

And if you love kids—even better. Serve in preschool. Come alongside children with special needs to give their parents a break. Invest in the lives of teenagers who need positive role models.

Look for others who need relationships too. For example, serve seniors who may be lonely or isolated.

2. Live in gospel community. The body of Christ is your family. God has given us the church as a place of fellowship, companionship, and accountability. It provides the opportunity for companionship we all need and long for.

Perhaps more than ever, younger generations are skeptical and critical of the church as an organization. Well, guess what? Organizations are imperfect because they're made up of broken people. Including you. If you're waiting for perfection, you won't find it—and you don't have it either. So invest yourself in a gospel community. Bring your influence to help make it the best it can be. Extend grace. Receive grace.

3. Participate and give to advance the Great Commission. You can engage in long-term or short-term mission work. You can go to another country, or get connected to internationals and refugees in your own community who have never heard the gospel.

And when it comes to giving—when you're single, you don't have to negotiate a budget with your spouse. So sit down and create your own spending plan. Line it up with biblical priorities. Either you tell your money where to go, or your money will tell you where it went. Pay down debt. Make responsible choices. Most importantly, invest financially in the kingdom of God.

In all these ways, we come full circle back to 1 Corinthians 7:17, where this chapter began:

Only let each person lead the life that the Lord has assigned to him, and to which God has called him.

God is sovereign over every season. Do you really believe that? Or are you like Abraham and Sarah, asking, *God, are you sure you've got this?*

Rest assured, he's got this.

Embrace God's purpose for you.

No matter your relationship status, you can find your identity in Christ. You don't need somebody in order to be somebody. And if you've found somebody, be grateful—but don't expect them to fulfill you in ways that Christ alone can.

You are complete in him.

Embrace God's purpose for you.

A Single Purpose

If you're single, commit to living the present with the future in view. In any dating relationship, keep Christ at the center. Pursue integrity, purity, and holiness as a foundation you can build on.

Who you *are* is more important than who you're *with*.

Embrace God's purpose for you.

And finally, make the most of every opportunity. That's the simple definition of stewardship. Whether you're married or single, live and share the grace of the gospel.

Let your light shine.

Embrace God's purpose for you.

Every one of us longs for a relationship that will change our life, not just our relationship status. The only one who can do that is Jesus Christ. Through him and by the Holy Spirit, the grace of the gospel lives at home within us.

Christ, our Savior,
We belong to you, heart and soul.
In you, we are complete.
We are loved unconditionally.
We are redeemed now and forever.
Give us grace to live as God has called us
and to trust that he is sovereign in every season.
Amen.

Eight
==

THE NEW NORMAL

Say the word "home" and it brings up all kinds of different images for different people. Maybe you picture your childhood home and the backyard where you once played. Maybe you envision a dream home you saw in a magazine or found on Zillow.

Or perhaps your image of home is more sobering. You're thinking of the honey-do list of chores and repairs you never have time for. Or piles of laundry. Or the argument you had in the kitchen last night. Or the side of the bed left empty by someone who's no longer with you.

Home is complicated.

It's where we live—not merely the shelter of four walls and a roof, but the place of hopes and dreams for ourselves and for those we love. The problem is, reality hits home when our marriage and family relationships bring us face-to-face with our brokenness. Hopes are diminished. Dreams are dashed. And we are left to wonder:

Will he ever be willing to reconcile?
Will she ever trust me again?

Can we recover from this setback?
Will our children grow up to make good choices?
How much longer must I pray for this season of struggle to end?
Will the pain of loss ever go away?

Questions like these point to a bittersweet truth—that even when we allow the grace of the gospel to enter and dwell in us, the brokenness we experience at home may not be fully restored in this life.

We might not be fully delivered.
We might not receive the healing we long for.
We might continue to experience pain and hardship.

Oh, there can be joy too. And laughter. And accomplishments, celebrations, milestones, and many wonderful moments. But ultimately, home is not about the fulfillment of our hopes and dreams.

No, home is the place where God daily reveals his purpose and glory in and through us—and this is the promise of the gospel. Without Christ, we face brokenness without a remedy. But in Christ, we can look forward to redemption.

This is the new normal.

God's Word anchors us in the new normal. It shines the light of truth on our path. And while it doesn't change our hard circumstances, it changes us—it changes our perspective.

So, in this chapter, we're going to look at important truths that transform us as we live in the new normal. Specifically, we will explore the words of the apostle Paul in 2 Corinthians 12:7 to 10.

Before we read these verses, we need to be aware of the context. It references some of the good things God has done through Paul's ministry. Paul could brag if he wanted to, but he does the opposite. He writes about his weaknesses:

The New Normal

So to keep me from becoming conceited because of the surpassing greatness of the revelations, a thorn was given me in the flesh, a messenger of Satan to harass me, to keep me from becoming conceited.

Three times I pleaded with the Lord about this, that it should leave me. But he said to me, "My grace is sufficient for you, for my power is made perfect in weakness." Therefore I will boast all the more gladly of my weaknesses, so that the power of Christ may rest upon me.

For the sake of Christ, then, I am content with weaknesses, insults, hardships, persecutions, and calamities. For when I am weak, then I am strong.

Paul is honest here. He's not keeping up appearances. His words are vulnerable and transparent. He acknowledges a thorn in his flesh—a struggle that keeps him humble.

Imagine a splinter in the bottom of your foot. It may be small and unseen by anyone. But it inflicts pain. Every step drives it deeper. It's a thorn in the flesh.

Paul admits a difficulty but doesn't tell us what it is. All we know is the struggle it causes in his life. He doesn't like the situation. He wants it to change.

Some people think it may have been an eyesight issue or physical disability. Others suggest a temptation that would not go away. Or maybe it was the opposition he faced everywhere he went; people questioned his apostleship and wanted to kill him. Or it could have been spiritual oppression.

Maybe it's a good thing we don't know what the thorn is. We know all we need to know: It was difficult.

Paul uses strong words: "It was sent to *harass* me." That word can be translated "to beat with a fist." So he's saying that the thorn in his flesh was beating him down. It was wearing him out.

Are you experiencing a hardship like that?

The tough reality sets in for Paul—and possibly for you too—when God doesn't remove the thorn. So what now? How are you going to cope with this new normal? To find out, let's carefully examine the verses we've just read and find four truths God has for us today.

In the new normal, there is purpose in your pain.

First, we find in verse 7 that God has allowed the thorn in the flesh to keep Paul from becoming excessively proud. This is so important that Paul says it twice:

> So *to keep me from becoming conceited* because of the surpassing greatness of the revelations, a thorn was given me in the flesh, a messenger of Satan to harass me, *to keep me from becoming conceited.*

The thorn is a constant reminder to depend on God's grace. No amount of self-reliance or self-sufficiency can overcome this hardship.

Apparently, there are enough good things happening in Paul's ministry that he could have bragged and said: *Hey, look at me and all I have done.* But because of the thorn in his flesh, he recognizes there's no human reason for the good things to happen. All the glory goes to Christ.

In our lives, it would be easy to think that the things we do are because of our strength, our ability, or our giftedness. Yet, God allows suffering in our lives to remind us that we are dependent upon him.

We see this same idea in a story found in John 9:1 to 3, which describes a conversation between Jesus and his disciples about a blind man:

The New Normal

> As [Jesus] passed by, he saw a man blind from birth. And his disciples asked him, "Rabbi, who sinned, this man or his parents, that he was born blind?" Jesus answered, "It was not that this man sinned, or his parents, but that the works of God might be displayed in him."

Do you see what's happening here? The disciples are looking at this man's pain. They're looking at his struggle, and they're asking the same questions that many of us ask when we face hardship we don't understand.

What caused this condition?
Whose sin brought this punishment?

The disciples assume that the man's blindness is a consequence of sin. Before we get too concerned that the disciples are out of line for equating sin with disability, we need to note something about the religious elite at the time of Jesus. They equated sickness with punishment from God.

So this is a reasonable conversation for the disciples to have with Jesus. They simply want to know the cause of this man's blindness. They know it wasn't due to an accident, so it must be something else—something more significant.

When Jesus hears the question from his disciples, he responds by shifting their focus from *cause* to *purpose*. And the purpose is that the works of God might be displayed in him.

We struggle when reality differs from our hopes and dreams.

What did I do to deserve this?
Is God punishing me for something?

We question the cause, but God points us to the purpose. Still, even when the new normal is hard to accept, God doesn't waste our pain. Scripture assures us that the works of God are being displayed in us when we endure hardship.

For the blind man, the story in John 9 has a happy ending. Jesus enables the man to see for the very first time in his life—not because Jesus is obligated to do so, but because he seeks to reveal God's glory. He's pointing us to the purpose in pain.

What does this mean for you?

Maybe you're divorced; nobody plans on that.
Maybe you're a single parent.
Maybe you're desperate to be married.
Maybe you're married but miserable.
Maybe life has run off the rails—your kids, your career, whatever it is.

Here's the hope of the new normal: God is at work for your good and for his glory. There is purpose in your pain, regardless of whether healing or restoration comes sooner or later—or not until eternity.

You're at ground zero with a limited perspective. God has the 30,000-foot view. You can't possibly see what he sees. But as you grapple with the new normal—the persistent reality of brokenness and pain—the question is not about the cause.

The question is about the purpose. How can you learn to look for it? How can you learn to embrace it instead of second-guessing it? You'll see in 2 Corinthians 12:8 what Paul learned through prayer.

In the new normal, prayer is the pathway to clarity.

In Paul's words, you can feel the agony and desperation caused by the thorn in the flesh: "Three times I pleaded with the Lord about this, that it should leave me."

The New Normal

Three times.

Not three prayers, but more likely three different *seasons* of prayer.

And Paul *pleaded* with the Lord. He begged God for deliverance. He got on God's case about it. Urgently. Earnestly. Intensely. Paul was desperate for God to remove the thorn.

God, please . . .

We are reminded of another desperate prayer—of Jesus in the garden of Gethsemane. Mark's gospel records that Jesus prayed to the Father repeatedly, pleading to be spared the suffering that awaited him. Luke's gospel adds more details to the story; it says Jesus was in such agony that he sweat drops of blood, and an angel appeared from heaven to strengthen him.

What do we learn from this pleading with God?
That it's okay to be honest with God about how you feel.
That it's okay to pray fervently for suffering to end.
That it's okay to beg God for healing.

God, please . . .

Scripture tells us we have a wide-open opportunity to pray with confidence. In Hebrews 4:15 to 16 we read:

For we do not have a high priest who is unable to sympathize with our weaknesses, but one who in every respect has been tempted as we are, yet without sin. Let us then with confidence draw near to the throne of grace, that we may receive mercy and find grace to help in time of need.

Jesus, our high priest, understands our weakness. He understands our pain. There's no trial, no suffering in which Jesus can't say to you, *I've been there too*—because Jesus was on his knees in the garden of Gethsemane, pleading with the Father.

God, please . . .

And yet, in Romans 8:32, we read that God "did not spare his own Son but gave him up for us all. . . ." Jesus endured the cross so that the hope of the gospel would be available to us.

When we return to 2 Corinthians 12:9, we find that Paul endured suffering too, despite his desperate, pleading prayers. God did not answer by providing relief from pain, but by providing clarity in the midst of pain: *My grace is sufficient for you, for my power is made perfect in weakness.*

In this instance, God says no.

I'm not changing your circumstances.
This is the new normal.
The pain isn't going away.
But I'm not going away either.

And did you hear the purpose?
For my power is made perfect in weakness.

At times, we see God display his power by sustaining us *through* the situation rather than delivering us *from* the situation. And when we review these three situations in Scripture—of the blind man, Jesus, and Paul—we see in each one how God answered differently.

The blind man receives sight.
Jesus receives an angel.
Paul receives perspective.

But what is the same about all three? God receives glory.

Here's the thing we have to understand: Prayer is about more than changing our circumstances. It's about changing us. It's about transforming our hearts. Prayer brings clarity about something we can't live without—grace.

In the new normal, God's grace is enough for you.

Paul had prayed and pleaded with God three times. Now look again at God's answer to him: *My grace is sufficient for you.*

That's it.

That simple.

And for Paul, it's a game-changer, because God's grace means everything to him. Paul remembers who he once was—a pious Jewish leader named Saul, hostile to Christians, who encountered the blinding glory of God in one of the most dramatic conversion experiences recorded in the Bible.

We read in the book of Acts that Saul was on the road to Damascus. He had official papers in hand that authorized the imprisonment and murder of Christians. Saul hated Jesus. He was an enemy of the gospel.

Then, out of nowhere, came a light and a voice from heaven. "Saul, Saul, why are you persecuting me?"

In that moment, Saul deserved nothing more than judgment and wrath. But grace changed everything. His faith. His eyesight. Even his name: He became Paul. And the zeal he once expressed against Christ became fuel for a life devoted to Christ.

Paul never forgot the grace of God and where it found him.

My grace is sufficient for you.

The same grace that was more than enough to forgive your sin.

The same grace that was more than enough to transform your heart.

The same grace that is more than enough to sustain you through the season of life you're in.

My grace is sufficient for you.

My—that's God saying, *I've got this. I'll bring it.*

Grace—that's favor you didn't earn and don't deserve, given freely.

Is—present tense. Now. Right this second. In this very moment and in every moment today, tomorrow, the next day, and the day after that. The day you're ready to call it quits. The day you get devastating news. The day you feel like there's no turning back and no path forward. My grace *is*.

Is what? *Sufficient.* That means enough. It's daily manna from heaven to feed your soul. Enough to sustain you through whatever struggle you're facing. Enough to cover your sin and shame. Enough to redeem you from the worst failure you can possibly imagine.

Hear God's promise for you today: *My grace is sufficient for you.* Open your Bible to 2 Corinthians 12:9 and mark that phrase. Mark it in your heart.

How much grace is that? How do you know it will be enough? Look at Romans 8:31 to 32, where Paul writes:

What then shall we say to these things? If God is for us, who can be against us? He who did not spare his own Son but gave him up for us all, how will he not also with him graciously give us all things?

Paul says that if God demonstrated his grace by sending Jesus to die on a cross, to give up his life for ours, then how much more is he willing to give us the grace we need to sustain us day by day?

Rest in this truth.

The grace that saves you is the same grace that sustains you.

The grace that makes you a child of God is the same grace that enables you to live as a child of God through the struggle and sorrow you face.

My grace is sufficient for you. And that's even not the end of the verse—*for my power is made perfect in weakness.*

The New Normal

In the new normal, God's power is perfected in weakness.

Did you notice that grace and power come from the same source? *My* grace. *My* power. We can trust both.

When we come to a place of weakness, when we have lost all strength, when we realize we have nothing left to give—God's power is not only available to us, it is *made perfect* in us.

The power of the one crucified on Friday and resurrected on Sunday.
The power of the one victorious over sin and death and hell.
That power.
And it's still in the present tense. My power *is*.

Think about it: When someone is too weak to carry a burden, there are two ways to deal with it. One is to remove the burden. The other is to provide the strength needed to carry on—and when God does that, the world sees his divine power at work in our marriage and family. It's an opportunity to showcase the gospel in the home.

Even Jesus accepted weakness in order to show God's power. Although Jesus possessed all power in heaven and on earth, he traded it for the weakness of being born in human flesh. He humbled himself to the point that he was put to death on a cross. His dead body was placed in a tomb. But three days later, weakness gave way to power—God's power displayed to demonstrate the hope of the gospel.

Paul writes in Romans 1:16: "For I am not ashamed of the gospel, for it is the power of God for salvation to everyone who believes"—power made more evident in contrast to human weakness.

To embrace the power of the gospel, you have to come to the realization of your weakness.

I'm broken.
I can't fix myself.

I can't redeem myself.
My strength isn't enough.

And that, God says, is where his power comes in. The gospel comes in. It transforms who you are. It brings you to a place of humility, where you recognize: *The only strength I have is found in Jesus. The only power I have is found in Christ.*

This is the paradox of power perfected in weakness.
This is the mystery of grace revealed in brokenness.
This is the new normal.

As you live in this new normal, you have the opportunity to respond as Paul did in 2 Corinthians 12:9 to 10, which says:

Therefore I will boast all the more gladly of my weaknesses, so that the power of Christ may rest upon me. For the sake of Christ, then, I am content with weaknesses, insults, hardships, persecutions, and calamities. For when I am weak, then I am strong.

Notice that last statement. *For when I am weak, then I am strong.* Paul is not saying he used to *feel* weak and but now he *feels* strong. No. Circumstances haven't changed; they're still difficult. But when *I am* weak, then *I am* strong.
Present tense.
Because God's grace *is*, because God's power *is*, therefore *I am*.

The gospel is a "present tense" reality!
Of course, you look back with joy on the day you were saved. You remember the excitement of the day you were baptized. But don't get stuck in past tense.
And of course, you look forward to heaven and to the experience

The New Normal

of ultimate restoration in Christ. But don't get stuck in future tense either.

Today and every day, you can experience the grace and power of God in your life. Now. No matter what you're facing.

• • •

For us, this book is present tense. It is not theoretical. It is not just a theological statement. We are living what we share with you in every chapter. And this chapter is no different.

So we have chosen to conclude with a personal story—an example to encourage you as you seek to live the new normal in your home.

Connor and Mary Bales: Our New Normal

When we speak about the gospel in the home, we speak from our experience. God has moved in our hearts and in our family to reveal his grace and power in our own "new normal."

Y'all wouldn't have known if you saw us starting out as a married couple that we would have such an extraordinary journey. But we have—and we are still on it.

Our life as newlyweds looked pretty typical. We both started our careers and advanced in those. Then we started our family a few years later. We were living what you might describe as a charmed life.

We welcomed our first daughter, Kathryn.

Then along came our first son, Coleman.

Connor had started a landscaping business and then successfully sold it to a much larger company. We were earning more income than we ever thought possible. We had bought the "forever home" of our dreams, and things were settling in very nicely for us.

Sounds picture-perfect, right?

Both of us were active in church, faithfully serving in student ministry, and we absolutely loved it. Each of us was leading a student Bible study—Connor for a group of boys, and Mary for a group of girls. We continued serving in this ministry until our respective groups finished high school. It was such a sweet time.

As is often the case, God used this season to grow and prepare us for more than we knew was coming our way.

During this particular season, God had spoken to Connor very clearly through the Holy Spirit. God had said, *I want you to sell your business, because I have called you to ministry.*

We joke now about Connor's mature response: He panicked. Then he waffled for a while. He considered enrolling in seminary. And finally, after about a year, he said *yes* to God.

You may recall our conversation at the end of chapter six where Mary talked about selling our "forever home." That was a big step of faith and obedience for us. We packed up our lives and our two small children and moved into an apartment.

In the meantime, Mary became pregnant with our third child—another girl. We decided to name her Libby.

By the fall of 2008, Connor was working full time and taking seminary classes at night and online. Libby was due in November. We had not yet done much preparation for her birth—after all, this was our third time around.

But we'll never forget one Monday morning when Mary thought it would be a good idea to get a few of the baby toys down from the attic. Connor climbed up, got the toys, and was coming back down when Mary said, "I think I'm going into labor."

"No way. Really?"

The baby wasn't due for another month. But just to be safe, we called the doctor to rule out any concerns. Come in for an exam, he said.

Well, that same afternoon, Libby was born. Early. And the moment she arrived, something was clearly wrong. Her feet weren't right. Now when he talks about that moment, Connor calls them *funky feet*. They were facing outward and pointing upward.

Normally—as you know if you've had a baby—the medical staff

The New Normal

immediately takes the newborn to check vitals. Then, after a good cry and a quick clean-up, the baby is placed in her mama's arms as daddy leans in to embrace them both.

But with Libby, the medical staff was busy doing so many things; they never handed her over. Without saying much to either of us, they took Libby away.

About an hour later, someone asked Connor if he would like to come see Libby. He followed them to the Neonatal Intensive Care Unit (NICU). And there was little Libby, hooked up to all kinds of machines. Connor stood in a fog of emotion and confusion.

The doctor explained the attempts to stabilize her breathing and regulate her body. But Connor couldn't hear through the fog.

By day two, the doctor had detected an irregular heartbeat in Libby. After testing and review of her condition by a pediatric cardiologist, we were informed that Libby would need to have heart surgery to repair a congenital defect.

Remember, we weren't even prepared for Libby to arrive by her due date, not to mention early—and now this. We were devastated.

Why is this happening to us?

But Libby was a strong baby. She only spent two weeks in the NICU. After we got home, we began our 'new normal' routine of appointments with her pediatrician and cardiologist. Cautiously, we began to interview cardiothoracic surgeons; Libby's surgery would be scheduled about the time of her first birthday. A year of life would give her heart—about the size of her fist—a chance to grow larger. That would make surgery easier and more likely to be successful.

Then, we figured we had time to adjust to the scary idea of heart surgery. Except that in our weekly appointments with the cardiologist, Libby's condition was found to be more severe than anticipated.

Not long ago, Connor was telling a young dad how he always did the midnight *SportsCenter* feeding with Libby. Since *SportsCenter* was on TV at midnight, he would watch while she took her bottle. And every night, her body was working so hard to eat, and her heart was functioning so inefficiently, that she would sweat through her onesie. Not a good sign.

> The doctor moved her surgery up from one year to six months.
> Then to 90 days.
> Then to next week.

So, at just 10 weeks of age, Libby went in for open-heart surgery.

As you can imagine, we were terrified. We handed her to the anesthesiologist, wondering whether or not she would survive.

In that moment, we sounded like the disciples, asking:

Why was she born this way?
What did we do to deserve this?

Looking back, we can see how God was good to our family and to Libby in particular. Through the skilled hands of the surgeons and medical team that cared for Libby, her surgery was a complete success.

While Libby was recovering in the hospital, some of the doctors suggested extra testing to be done on Libby. Evidently they had seen some things they wanted to monitor a bit more closely. That sounded like a good idea to us, because we were confident that once we got Libby's heart repaired, everything else would be fine.

Connor even told one of the doctors, "Listen, once we get the heart taken care of, I'll be asking you to fix her feet, because I really want Libby to look cute in her prom shoes."

As the doctor began to examine Libby's feet, he stepped back to get a good overall look at her. And we could see that his mental wheels were turning. Something else was not right.

The following month, a geneticist called and asked to meet with us. She had been the doctor who oversaw Libby's extra testing. She told us that Libby had a very rare chromosomal abnormality called trisomy 16p.

The New Normal

Libby would never walk.
Libby would never talk.
Libby would not learn to recognize us, her mama and daddy.
Libby would not live to see her second birthday.

We were surrounded by fog again.
"Is this like Down Syndrome?" we asked.
"Oh, Mr. and Mrs. Bales, this is so much more severe," the doctor said.

The doctor gave us as much information as possible—all of the statistical data that was available for such a rare condition.

We were undone.
Why was she born this way?

We were in shock.
What did we do to deserve this?

We were angry.
God, where are you?

We were angry even though we knew better:
No, this isn't punishment.
No, we aren't to blame.
And no, we can't fix it.

The new normal was settling in. We'd sold the business and our dream home. We'd moved into an apartment. Connor was in seminary. Mary was home with three little ones, including Libby and her special needs. The charmed life was long gone.

We felt helpless.

About six months after Libby's diagnosis, Connor was doing a devotional one morning in John, chapter 9:

> As [Jesus] passed by, he saw a man blind from birth. And his disciples asked him, "Rabbi, who sinned, this man or his parents, that he was born blind?" Jesus answered, "It was not that this man sinned, or his parents, but that the works of God might be displayed in him."

He already knew the story. But on this particular morning, he discovered something entirely different in it. The disciples' questions became more real and made more sense than ever before.

We began to understand that our new normal would allow the works of God to be displayed in our lives. But we didn't realize that life was about to get even more complicated.

We wrestled with our family's new normal. The season of anger, hurt, and grief was not easy or short. And on top of that, we had to adjust to Libby's line-up of medical care appointments, therapies, surgeries, and several unexpected hospital stays. All of these are part of life with this special little girl.

And Libby lived to see her second birthday.

Not long after that, we wanted to try again for another baby. We had been assured of the mathematical impossibilities of trisomy 16p, and we'd already had our one in however many million.

We were thrilled but also somewhat reserved to learn that we were expecting again. This time, Mary got all kinds of special care, just to make sure things were okay. We learned that Mary was pregnant with another little girl. We decided to name her Hannah.

Pregnancy with Hannah was smooth sailing. No complications. No alarms. Everything normal. Our anxiety faded as we prepared for her arrival.

But when Hannah was born, we knew something wasn't right. Oh, her feet were just as they should be, and the doctors couldn't detect any heart murmur. But still, something wasn't right.

Because of our family's history and some things the doctors had seen, there were good reasons to have Hannah tested.

A month later, we got the news: Hannah *did* have the exact same chromosomal abnormality as her sister Libby, trisomy 16p. The discovery was so rare that the head off the laboratory personally called our doctor to relay the information, after having run the tests twice to validate their accuracy.

In that moment, we were devastated all over again.

But this time something was different for us. As we sat in the car, in the parking lot of the doctor's office, the Holy Spirit spoke as clearly that day as when he called Connor into ministry: *I have counted you worthy to get to do this twice.*

It seems very unusual—but no more unusual than what Jesus replied to the disciples: *That the works of God might be displayed.*

Believe us, we have pleaded with God to realign the chromosomes of our little girls. We know that would take a work of God—and we would give him all the glory for it. But it's likely that their healing is not going to happen on this side of heaven; we're probably going to outlive them both. But God's work has already begun. His work in our new normal is active right now.

Are there moments when we grieve? You bet. Having your little girl airlifted more than a hundred miles to emergency care will make any parent shed tears.

Are there times when we're angry? For sure. We've been begging Jesus for two years to take Hannah's seizures away.

Are there moments when we're scared? Absolutely. Every time a doctor calls and won't tell us over the phone what the conversation needs to be about.

Is God working in every one of those moments? Yes.

You see, the work of God in our girls has caused our faith to grow—so much that we don't know where our faith would be if it weren't for them.

If that's not the work of God, then we don't know how to describe it.

There are therapists, teachers, and doctors who are hearing the good news of the gospel—which they might not otherwise hear—as they see our family's story play out.

If that's not the work of God, then we don't know how to describe it.

There are people in our church who have come to a saving relationship in Jesus Christ through the testimony of our girls who can't even speak a word.

If that's not the work of God, then we don't know how to describe it.

One of those people is Libby's caregiver, who did not have a relationship with the Lord when we hired her. She fell in love with Libby, which is easy to do if you know our girl. Then we began to have opportunities for spiritual conversations.

One night, the caregiver had a dream that Libby ran up to her—even though Libby doesn't walk. In the dream, Libby threw her arms around the caregiver and said, *I love you*—except Libby doesn't talk. Through that dream, Libby's caregiver believed that God was providing a picture of what redemption looks like.

If that's not the work of God, then we don't know how to describe it.

Doctors told us that Libby would not live to see her second birthday. But so far, we have celebrated seven birthdays with Libby, and four with Hannah.

If that's not the work of God, then we don't know how to describe it.

The New Normal

• • •

Here's the bottom-line truth about the new normal:
Jesus didn't die to give us a better life.
He died to give us an eternal one.

Jesus doesn't promise an end to our struggles.
He promises hope that goes beyond them.

My grace is sufficient for you, for my power is made perfect in weakness.

Present tense.
Today.
Now.

You can experience the hope of the gospel in your home as God's grace dwells in you and his power works through your weakness. It is sufficient. It is custom fit—exactly what you need, when you need it.

Gracious and powerful God,
Give us courage to face our new normal
with confidence that there is purpose in our pain.
Open our eyes and our hearts
to your work in and through us
to show the world the hope of the gospel.
Amen.

www.ingramcontent.com/pod-product-compliance
Lightning Source LLC
LaVergne TN
LVHW041542070426
835507LV00011B/888